Ice Cold Love

By Michael D McAuley

Internet dating is probably one of the modern world's most interesting romantic phenomena. When you hit the spot you can get it just right. There are pitfalls and dangers at every turn. Increasingly the internet is full of timewasters, nutcases not to mention some outright psychopaths. When you get it right you can find happiness just as well online as you may in a bar, or even the local supermarket. If ever there was one man who could tell you how not to meet people on the internet, one guy who could give you the do's and don'ts on internet dating, you would need to look no further than a sleepy suburban area of Birmingham called Kings Norton. There, just before the days of social media and before the likes of Facebook, or Twitter, even existed you would find a slim, short dark haired twenty-something man with all the experiences you could need to write an idiots guide on the subject. All you would have to do is ask Joe Hughes.

Let's start at the beginning of the tale as good stories often do. Before the fiery passion that almost consumed him at a time before he had met Loren.

Joe was at a cross roads in his life. He had recently left his wife Isobel after five long dramatic years, along with their young son Reece, and was back in the place he once called home. Living for what he hoped would only be a temporary basis in the caravan outside his parents 3 bed roomed house he felt like a bachelor for the first time in his life.

He found he had been released from a prison of his own making. After all had he really ever been stuck where he was, no Joe didn't think so. Joe just felt comfortable and scared of changed. He always knew it to be true but never wanted to move away, break out of the safety net of the life that had been given to him. There was of course his son Reece who he had looked after and watched fall asleep each night and that perhaps was this lock that had kept him bound.

Still it wasn't like he didn't get to see Reece anymore. He still got to see him at weekends. The time he spent with his son who had by then just turned four was quality time. Joe would take his little man as he called him and do his best to treat him like a King. Yes he spoiled him but the time he had with his son had grown short, so when Reece asked for sweets he got them. When Reece wanted to go to the cinema they went. Joe would always take him out to a fancy restaurant as though dining some fine lady. Joe would order up a fine meal for himself with a side order of Jack Daniels. Only one as one didn't hurt, as Joe didn't drive it really wasn't wrong of him to have a glass of his favourite tipple. In the presence of his son Joe never had more than one. Eventually after haggling on price with his brother Gary, Joe was able to get his son a computer games console. In hindsight not one of his brighter ideas but the small black box that was called a game cube would keep Reece out of mischief for hours at a time. Watching his son play the complicated looking video games Joe marvelled at how rapidly Reece picked up how to play all the games he bought him. It was amazing how he seemed to just take everything in so fast. Still Joe thought to himself at the time, a child's mind is like a sponge at such a young age.

So it was that after a five year relationship with Isobel Samson he found himself back living with his parents. He had his own space in the form of the small caravan that was located on their front drive. The setting was ideal for Joe. He had all the basic commodities he needed. In the small space of the caravan he had a fridge to keep any alcoholic beverages he would buy, not that he needed to store his favourite tipple of Jack Daniels in the fridge, but he did need somewhere to keep the wine chilled for the ladies and Joe knew there would be a lot of ladies to entertain. He had full working electricity in the caravan, not that he ever found himself watching much TV. If he wasn't entertaining as he called it he would just settle down with a good book and a glass of Jack Daniels and coke. As far as other facilities mattered if Joe wanted to shower, wash or even go to the toilet he had to go into the house. It was a small price to pay for his freedom. Still he did have a bucket for emergencies and Joe wasn't materialistic. It became his home for a long time, and the ladies did indeed frequent the caravan in plentiful supply. He met them all online. Joe kept the same honest approach he had while with Isobel always telling the women he met he just wanted some none serious fun. Occasionally someone would come along and he would try to form a relationship. He just never seemed to meet anyone that understood him well enough for him to make a real go of things.

There was a young teacher who just didn't get Joe's sarcastic humour, kept insisting he quit smoking. It turned out she still lived with her ex-partner. If she really was split from him Joe thought laughing as he moved onto the next woman. There were some really awful women; big, hairy or just plain gorgeous and crazy, Joe slept with them all before showing them the door.

He had regained his freedom. He was content for a very long time. He had no wish to settle down after such a long relationship with Isobel. Joe would see Reece at weekends. One week he would look after him during the day then the following week he would have him from Saturday afternoon until Sunday morning. It was a perfect set up. He still got to see his son. He was able to work the occasional bit of Saturday overtime, not to mention go out every other Saturday night with his mates if he so chose to do so. He even joined a gym for a short time. He hoped it would widen his social circle. He had been very keen on physical fitness in his younger days working out in the darkness of his parent's garage every night of the week.

    All in all Joe Hughes had a very full life. His caravan was never short of lady or a beer. Reece was always kept happy with trips out for meals, or to the cinema, or was even just happy watching DVD's with his dad at his grandparents. During the summer Reece would stay in the caravan on the night's he stopped over. The young boy loved it. It was all part of a big adventure for him. Still after a while Joe got tired of seeing all the different women. He met one woman who was more hairy than Chewbacca from Star Wars, finding that he was running from her house. He even had sex with a woman out in an open field up in Coventry while people played football nearby. He felt like he was becoming addicted to his internet sex. Still he carried on hoping that he would meet someone that would sway him away from his ludicrous ways. He wanted nothing more than someone in his life that could understand him. Neither Katrina nor Isobel had ever really had anything in common with him. They had been the longest relationships of his life, but he found he was happy with his one night stands as they expected little of him, and yet seemed to accept him for the person he was.

After three months of this Joe eventually met up with a girl that was just off the rails. She was a looker for sure, but also as mad as the Hatter from Wonderland. The young girl who gave herself the unbelievable name of Cassandra had a nervous twitch, not to mention an attention span that was only equalled by that of his four year old son. She had come down for the weekend. As soon as Joe met her he wanted her to leave, but she had come all the way from Shropshire supposedly. He spent a frightening night with the woman in his caravan, before unavoidable taking her with him when he went to pick up Reece. It all ended with her attacking him when Reece accidentally got mud on her new sneakers. The police had just walked past. This was the last straw for Joe's internet dating. He ran with his son in his arms, never looked back, never saw the strange woman with the twitch again.

By then Joe had no idea how many women he had slept with. He couldn't remember half their names let alone anything else about them. He actually felt ashamed even though the friends he had that believed his wild stories told him his was a legend. That was men for you.

For several weeks Joe kept off the various chat websites he had been visiting. He was very fearful that he would bump into someone else just as psychotic as the last woman. He still used his PC on a daily basis for playing games or selling some of his old comic book collection on Ebay. He had no intention of meeting anyone else for a long time. Still it was all an addiction. Joe didn't really have much will power in regards to his return to the sites. One site in particular was Chatsmart. After a while he found himself logging on again.

One day while browsing the various profiles he came across a picture of a stunningly beautiful woman. He looked at the photograph. He laughed. The woman whose name according the profile was Loren was way out of his league. She was attractive, single, and as he read on very much like him. She had a love for Nicolas Cage, one of Joe's own personal favourite actors. She seemed to have a sarcastic streak in her sense of humour or so the profile told him. So Joe decided it would do no harm in messaging the woman. After all he had nothing to lose. She would either reply or not. So he sent her a message telling her all about how they shared the same favourite actor as well as sense of humour. He left his email for chat at the bottom letting her know that if she wanted to add him he was on chat most nights. Joe eventually messaged around half a dozen women not caring if he got a response from any of them least of all the Nicolas Cage fan that seemed so like him. He just wasn't too keen on meeting anyone else so soon after his brush with the crazy woman.

Several days went by with each passing one pulling Joe further into the chat addiction he thought he had beaten. Still he was doing well as he hadn't agreed or even asked to meet up with anyone else since the last time. No one was actually on chat one particular Saturday afternoon, but Joe left the program running on the off chance that someone he knew would pop on to talk to him. He had made a good many female friends despite meeting a lot of women just for fun. He had no problem talking to his friends. Just then a new chatter suddenly appeared on his chat log. He didn't recognise the email and tried to figure out who it might be.

"Hello" typed the new chatter. The log on ID told him the woman's name. God help him he hoped it was a woman you never could tell with chat unless the person on the other end possessed a webcam.

"How's your weekend been?"

"Good ty, I came back off hols yesterday"

"Where did u go?" Joe enquired.

"Devon," The response came back.

"How was it?"

"We only had four days of sunshine out of two whole weeks."

"Better than none," typed Joe. ", British weather eh."

"You probably don't even know who I am...lol" she typed.

"I do you're the lovely lady off Chatsmart. The one that has a thing for Nicolas Cage and John Cusack," He typed back.

He was remembering how he had messaged a 34 year old woman by the name of Loren after spotting her picture on

Chatsmart a website he had used quite regularly to give out his email address to women. For the most part it had been to bed them with the exception of a few women who had become friends, such a Amanda the witch, and Alex the lovely girl who shared his taste for Genesis. This girl seemed to share his tastes in music and movies so he had emailed her intrigued to find out what she was really like.

"You have a good memory."

"I know."

"I'm impressed."

"Where you from again and are you still single as it says on your Chatsmart profile or have you met someone since you replied to my message?"

"Sutton Coldfield still single."

"Cool. Well if you like we could meet up as mates for a drink one evening. Take it nice and slow. I'm a bit apprehensive as the last person I met attacked me while I held my 4 year old son in my arms."

"You're joking. That's awful."

"Sadly not. It kind of makes me a bit wary. But being a crazy guy I don't give up."

"I'm in no rush. Never met anyone off the internet. There's a lot of weird people about."

"Tell me about it." Typed Joe thinking he must have met most of the female nutters available by now.

"Well Joe you seem like a nice bloke. Why are you looking on here?

"I'm shy in real life just meeting girls in bars. It just seems easier to get to know people this way."

This was of course true Joe had for the most part of his life been a very shy young man even after meeting Katrina, and later Isobel, there had been few women to come before them. Then after most of the women he had met he had met online. Joe just wasn't brave enough to go up to a woman in a bar and ask her for a number, more importantly he hated cheesy chat up lines; especially when he knew he didn't really have any of his own. So even though Joe had bedded more women than he could remember the names of, which faded from his memory like a fine mist he was still essentially the same shy bloke he had always been. Yes the internet helped him a great deal. Once he had taken to someone online it seemed to boost his confidence no end. When he eventually met people he had no problem cutting to the chase, after all for the most part both parties generally knew what they were after.

"It is easy yes," typed Loren. "People can pretend to be something they are not." Joe didn't realise then how much truth was in those typed letters that appeared on his screen.

"You don't expect people to be completely psycho though. I've met people before and made some good mates nothing like the last time."

"So you have met people off here a lot?"

"No comment." Typed Joe knowing the answer would surely put Loren off talking to him for good. What could he say really? Yes I have met loads of women and I have slept with most of them and then just said my goodbyes. Joe didn't figure that that kind of approach would go down too well. He saw the icon symbolizing that Loren did indeed have a webcam. Ordinarily he would have just invited her to put her camera on with the press of a button. Something was stopping him. Was it nerves? He didn't know. In truth at the time he didn't really think about it. He just knew it wasn't right. He had read the woman's description on Chatsmart. From what she had written she seemed to share a lot in common with him and be a very warm person. Also it had to be said from the picture displayed on her Chatsmart page the woman looked like a complete knockout. Perhaps not supermodel material but she seemed to have a natural beauty that most women could only dream of possessing. So Joe held back and didn't ask her to view his cam, or let him view hers. He simply sat back and waited for her to type her reply.

"I've never met anyone. I'm far too sensible for that. Well anyway I have to go now Joe. It was very nice chatting to you."

"Likewise," typed Joe and at that he gave her his number as it had always been the way, and she seemed harmless enough. Didn't they always.

It wasn't long before she came back of course it was later that same evening in fact. Joe had barely left his pc that day for even an hour only moving from his stool once to make himself a quick microwaveable curry. He was selling his old comic book collection on the auction website on Ebay and kept receiving numerous emails questioning him about the condition of one book or another. Then of course his friend Amanda had come onto chat. She was having a rough time with her boyfriend who she had recently found out actually had a wife in Leeds where he worked as a Salesman of sorts. Picking up the phone Joe did his best to listen to Amanda. He always knew it was good to get your problems out in the open. He had found he needed to do it himself more often than not and it took his mind off his own problems. He was glad to be able to be there for Amanda. It was around mid-afternoon just after he had got off the phone with Amanda that Loren came back online inviting him to view her webcam for the first time and asking him to do likewise with her. So through the online chat they both saw each other for the first time.

"Hellooooo," came the usual exaggerated typed opening

"Helloo Looooren," replied Joe.

"So what music are you into?"

"I like anything," Joe told her, "At the moment I'm listening to Usher, and really like a new band called Maroon 5. How about yourself?"

"I like most things from 60s through to current stuff. I like the odd song more than groups."

"If I like it I like it that's how I feel about music. I don't pigeon hole my tastes." Joe typed back

"Nor me I was playing Jolene earlier, then played you can't hurry love...big difference."

"My youngest decided he wasn't sleeping last night we watched Scooby Doo all night."

"Clever how they can make up their own minds like that. My son Reece is the same when I have him overnight. Still I don't mind letting him stay up as its more quality time for me."

"Tell me about it every time I closed my eyes he'd poke me telling me to watch the film. Before you ask he is 3. His name is Tim he starts nursery in September. Then there is Joss who is 5, Larry who is 11, and finally Harriet who is 13 going on 21 lol"

"So you have got a real Brady bunch there, "Joe joked.

"I have my hands full yes."

"My son Reece finished nursery Friday. He is four," typed Joe. He was glad to be able to share the joys and trails of parenthood with someone that seemed to understand. With every word he typed she beamed at him with amazing smile, while all the time playing with her shoulder length blonde hair.

"Smile," She typed.

"I hate smiling," He typed in response but gave her his goofiest I'm a really happy guy and so pleased to see you smile that he could muster. It became a little game with them in chats in the future. They both loved to see each other smile, loved to just sit there and look at each other online. For the moment though it was fresh and new. No troubles were in sight, but that was life. You eventually had to take the good with the bad.

"So what's your job exactly again?" Joe typed, "On Chatsmart you have put that you are a nurse."

"I work in theatre a lot. Sections"

"What you work in sections like you section nutters," he joked.

"No I mean caesarean sections. I work in a labour ward. Help out the doctors preparing the equipment and prepping things."

"Must be very rewarding"

"I love my job," she smiled at this.

"So have you never in anyway shape or form met anybody male or female off the net?"

"No. I'm not sure I would. I mean it's one thing chatting on here. This is all new to me. Most of my friends all chat online so I thought I'd give it a go to pass the time. Besides from what you tell me there are a lot of nutters out there like that woman that attacked you. Maybe I should heed your words and stick to chat,"

The look of sarcasm on Loren's face told Joe that she wasn't as apprehensive about meeting as she was letting on. That was good he really was warming to this woman and wanted to get to know her better.

"Give us a twirl," he typed trying his luck. He wanted to see what the rest of this fine sarcastic woman looked like. He looked at her on cam. He was amazed at how enraptured by her he felt.

"What are you looking at? You have a really serious expression on your face" she typed ignoring his request.

"I'm just staring,"

"What at me? I'm just little old me. Nothing special," at that she played with her hair again. "I'm just your average girl next door who loves to dance."

"Give us a twirl," he typed again. "Look I will do one myself in my crappy t-shirt"

At that Joe got of the stool he was sitting on and waved around his hands and did an awkward dance for the woman on camera. He knew he must have looked a complete prat. He didn't mind it was making the woman on the other end of the computer laugh. She had such a wonderful smile.

She laughed at this and got up typing as she did.

"Ok here goes." she said. At that she moved away from her computer revealing that she was wearing a short sleeved woollen top and corduroy pants. She looked beautifully normal. The one thing Joe loved the most was she seemed to smile all the time. Joe almost suspected she was enjoying showing herself and off to him. She gave Joe a slow motion twirl, having moved away from her laptop. Before also moving the camera around her sitting room pointing out various toys and video's her children loved to watch

"See there you go nothing special. Just little old me," she typed as she sat back down. Joe didn't agree though. She looked great in her normalness. Loren seemed a real genuine woman, perhaps the first genuine person he had met online in a long time.

"Ooh no. I give you ten out of ten. Then again that psycho I met was nice too, except for having a nervous twitch so I don't just judge people by their looks, and you do look amazing."

She blushed at this and her smile widened. "You're a lovely sweet man Joe. I think more than likely you're a great father too."

"So are you going to meet me?" Joe asked her.

"It's tempting," she replied. "Think I'd like to chat more first though. Funny I really like you. You don't seem like most people online. Most men are only after one thing.

Anyway I have your number so maybe I'll just surprise you one day."

"But I don't have your number," protested Joe

"No you don't," she smiled "Anyway I have to go again chat soon. Kids need me."

"Bye for now."

"Bye Joe."

They didn't chat again for several days. It did make Joe wonder. Loren had her life to lead, he had his. There were still plenty of people on chat for him to while away the hours with. During that time the weekend passed and he had Reece overnight. Picking his son up one Saturday afternoon as he always did when his son was spending the night he took him to a restaurant for his dinner. It was a place that sold chicken at the top of Broad Street that was just a few minutes from the cinema. After their meal that included several toilet trips for Reece and an insistence as per usual that he wanted to go home and play the Mario game on the game cube, they did go to the cinema, and got a bag of sweets for Reece which his dad informed he had to share. They watched a Disney movie entitled Shrek about a large Ogre voiced by Mike Myers that had to rescue a princess with the aid of a talking donkey who was voiced by Eddie Murphy. Reece laughed throughout which always made his dad smile. He loved nothing more than spending quality time with his little man. Since he split with Isobel all the moments he had with Reece at weekends were quality time. Reece eventually got what he wanted. His father did take him back to let him play the game cube for a few hours before tucking him up in bed and falling asleep beside him and then that was another weekend over as the following day he took him back to his mom.

It was then on the Sunday evening as Joe was chatting to several rather oddball women who seemed interested in only one thing, meeting up with him and having a good time. Joe realised he was no longer interested in that kind of thing. On splitting with Isobel he had spent three months of sowing his wild oats as he described it. He no longer had the heart to meet women off the internet for harmless fun. Joe was ready to meet someone that he could give more to. As he had hoped, Loren Green did pop back on chat that evening, as she did for several evenings after for the following two weeks. They chatted about their love of music and movies and often played guessing games on what movies starred their favourite actors. They would always finish each other's sentences then type 'snap' and look at each other and laugh before staring at each other and smiling for many minutes. Occasionally Loren would have to disappear as she always did, not surprising with four kids running around in the background. Joe had come accustomed to his chats with Loren and looked forward to each one. The more he found out about the beautiful woman that appeared on his screen playing, twirling with her shoulder length hair the more he felt at ease with her. They were both very much alike in every sense, something they agreed on whole heartedly as they swapped light hearted sarcastic insults. For a long while Joe suffered a head ache that wouldn't go away and Loren always told him how ill he looked and that he shouldn't be online chatting to her. No, she would tell him he should be tucked up in bed in a darkened room so that the headache could pass. To this Joe always joked he would do gladly if she would only join him. A nice idea she would tell him, but that is as far as their flirting ever went. He did hope she would get over her apprehension of internet dating despite all the scare stories of his own that he had shared with her, and meet him. He hoped that would be one day soon. So on that Sunday evening they chatted once more.

"I'd have to be mad to have 4 kids," she typed to him after their usual greeting of an extending hello. Yes he thought you probably do. With the amount of time she disappeared from the view of the camera though it was obvious she was a great mother. Loren's kids always came first

"Yes you would. Why, do you want more?" Joe joked.

"I used to. Don't know now. If I met someone and fell madly in love and was happy maybe."

"I know what you mean I never loved Reece's mom." Joe admitted. It wasn't something he had hidden from anyone, least of all Isobel. He hoped being honest with Loren wouldn't make her feel bad about him in anyway.

"What about you?" Loren typed.

"To be honest I don't know either? I'd like to be able to meet someone I can have an equal share of love with, and well humour is very important to me." He typed feeling at ease sitting on his stool in his parent's kitchen staring at her longingly as he had come to do. He loved looking at Loren. Okay maybe love was a strong word. He just couldn't get her out of his head. Whenever he closed his eyes he saw her face. It was infuriating, yet welcoming all the same.

"Me too," she typed back.

"Well I gave you my number so I must already trust you a tiny bit lol. No the fact is Psycho's do not have kids." He typed back with a real honesty with his words. With most women he had chatted to in the past online he always seemed to tell them what they wanted to hear. The whole idea being to get them into bed. With Loren things were different. He felt as though he could share anything with her, at least he hoped that would be the case.

"Well you're not setting a good example you know Joe."

"How do you mean?"

"Giving your number out to someone you've spoken to just a couple times."

"Well we get on really well. We both like Nicolas Cage and if you turn out be a nutter I just won't talk to you anymore lol."

"Ok then Joe I think maybe I'll just have to give you a call sometime."

As usual their conversation online ended quiet abruptly. Loren would appear to look at something out of his view. She seemed to be arguing with one of the kids about something are other. He never asked what. It wasn't any of his business. Still he knew he would listen to anything she wanted to tell him. So they did indeed keep chatting on many an occasion over the next few weeks.

Joe would always remember the first time she called. He had just been to Cotteridge to buy a CD for a new American band called maroon 5. Funny, whenever he listened to the tracks on the album entitled 'Songs about Jane' he seemed to think of Loren. The album seemed to be of great love but also of great heart ache. He had had enough of the latter but would gladly have received the first from Loren. He wanted nothing better than for her to be his Jane.

He was playing the CD on the stereo in his caravan. It was an Aiwa Hi-Fi system capable of storing 3 cds at once and playing them at random. He had bought it cheaply off a friend, and knew full well not to turn his speakers up too loud or he would hear a rather irritating buzzing sound. At any rate it had only cost him twenty pounds from his friend Amanda and added to the bachelor pad that his caravan had become. It was then as he listened to the tracks on his new album that his phone rang. It played on odd but catchy tune that was a standard mobile ring tone.

Joe didn't recognise the number at all. He picked up the phone and answered.

"Hello?" he said curious as to who might be calling him. In the past he had given his number out to many people online. But he hadn't given his number to many people recently. Then as the voice on the other end spoke he knew who it was.

"Hiya! How are you Joe?" came the reply in a soft voice he recognised instantly even though he had never heard it before in his life. It was her, it was Loren.

His whole body was shaking with excitement. He felt like a teenager rather than a young man only a few years from thirty"

"Loren?" he said knowing full well it was.

"That's right funny man," she laughed. "Who else would it be? I bet you have loads of girls calling you. I'm just at work and thought I'd say hello. So hello Joe."

She was right of course, and Joe felt an immediate pang of guilt for this woman he had never met. There were more than a dozen women's numbers stored on his mobile phone. Sure three or four of them were just good friends. However most of them were past conquests. Women he had met and bedded almost instantly. Still after the last person he had met he hadn't called up any of his conquests and any new numbers he had been given he had either deleted from his phone or just not bothered to contact. The last person he met he had made the unfortunate mistake of seeing while with his son and she had turned out to be a loony with a nervous twitch, a rising temper and far too much baggage for Joe to handle. That had all happened over a month ago, and now Loren was in his life. That he was content with. He had no intention of going back to his old ways. He had sowed his wild oats enough.

"So how's work?" Joe asked

"It's a bit quiet. Sometimes it's barmy here like me and other times we get quiet moments. My jobs like me, "she laughed adding, "you just never know. So what you been up to?"

"I have just been to buy a new CD."

"Who wasn't more into my sixties and seventies that current stuff?"

"Maroon 5," Joe told her.

"Think I have heard of them. They sing that song that's out now 'She will be loved' don't they?"

"Yep that's right. Apparently they were playing up town a few months back but I hadn't heard of them then. If I had known how good they were I would have gone and seen them.

"Oooh you could have taken me," she said

Joe could tell she was smiling as she spoke. He just knew it they both seemed to bounce off each other. It was just like how they were online only better. They talked for another ten minutes before Loren had to get back to her job, swapping music and movie tastes. That's when Joe told her about his past about all the women he had been with. It didn't faze her in the slightest. All she said was that she thought he was a nice man and it didn't bother her in the slightest how many women he had been with in the past. It was then as their conversation was drawing to a close that Joe told her what he wanted. What he hoped he would one day be able to give her.

"I just want to be happy for a change," he told her. "I'm tired of sleeping around and meeting bloody psychotic women off the internet. I want what they have in the movies that magical romance that should be part of real life."

"Well I'm definitely no psycho Joe," she said with that same infectious laughter that made him smile.

"No I don't for a minute believe you are."

"And for what it's worth Joe that's what I'd like too. You seem a lovely nice man and I'd really like to get to know you. Maybe just maybe you can show my little life some of that movie magic. God knows I need it."

"So meet me," he ventured.

"I will," she said, "Soon. I promise I will meet up with you for lunch when I'm not at work."

At that their conversation was ended as a buzzer in the background of Hope Springs where Loren worked sounded. They said their goodbyes and Joe knew they would talk again soon. After all she had told him to call her back in about half an hour. That he did and every hour or so after. They talked and chatted all evening until nine o'clock. She was on a late shift one o'clock in the afternoon till nine in the evening. The more they chatted the more they both found how alike they really were. It wasn't about shared interests but about two almost identical personalities. Sure they both enjoyed similar music, though Joe had a much wider taste than Loren, they liked many of the same actors, but it was more than that, they seemed to bounce off each other's every sentence as though their words were a song of their own making.

Joe didn't get out much. His social life was pretty non existent most of the time, especially as he had knocked the idea of internet tom foolery on the head. What with seeing Reece at the weekends he didn't really get much chance to get out when his friends were available, though once a month he would go see his mate Amanda who lived in Rubery. One Friday night a group of work colleagues had decided to go up town to celebrate his mate Bobby's Birthday. They were out all night drinking. Joe loved Jack Daniels so spent most of the night refilling his glass at the bar while joking with his friends. He always drank doubles, but dancing sobered him up. Joe wasn't much of a dancer but he did enjoy it. He just loved the way you could let go on the dance floor. He felt free when he danced not caring how bad he was at it just that he was enjoying himself. They started off in a few bars down Hurst Street. At one time there had been a rather large cinema complex down in the Arcadian, or what was known as the Chinese quarter, but it had long been closed down to be surrounded by over a dozen different bars catering to all tastes. In the end they headed to bar known as the academy, a place that played various styles of music from Indie to golden oldies.

As he danced the night away with his friends Joe found himself thinking of Loren he missed their online chats he missed hearing her voice on the phone. He decided to go to the men's where it was quiet to give her a quick call. He got the answering machine service. Why wouldn't he? He couldn't expect the woman to answer his calls all the time. She did after all have a life of her own. He left a message for her telling her how he was having a great night. He told her how much he wished she could be there at the Academy with him. With her love of music she would have really enjoyed a night out dancing with him. It would do her good to get out he thought. She probably didn't get out much he told himself. How could she? A single woman with four kids it wasn't really a very good situation to be in. Joe wondered where the father of her children was. He knew things could be hard. Relationships had a habit of going bad he knew that from his own experience. Still having left his message there was no more he could do. So with no answer he carried on dancing, knocked back more Jack Daniels yet every now and then he would try calling again or sent Loren a text. He had yet to meet her. He knew it was on the cards that it would happen. He just wished she was with him now.

    At around two thirty in the morning Joe and a handful of his friends decided it was time to call it a night. They had danced until the sweat poured from them ridding their bodies of any alcohol. They had, or at least Joe had, sang like loud crazy people. He knew if Loren had been with him she would have sang along just as loudly with him. The academy was open until three so the others wouldn't be far behind them. Catching individual taxi's as none of them lived anywhere near each other they all went their separate ways. Joe arrived home tired and weary. He had to be up early to pick up Reece. He was fine though. He was happy and went to sleep thinking of Loren.

The following morning Joe woke with a hangover. Going downstairs and making himself a strong cup of coffee he turned on his pc and checked his emails. Loren had sent him one. He read it with a feeling of unease creeping over him as he sipped at his cup of coffee.

'Good morning. How's your head? I've not been able to sleep last night because of thinking about you. I read your last messages. You've really fallen for me haven't you? As I keep telling you I like you as well. I know you'reconfused about what's going on with me so I'll tell you. My husband still lives here. We are not together. I don't love him haven't for years. I met him when I was 16yrs old and we just kind of stayed together. I'm looking for a house to rent because he won't move out! He says it's my decision to end the marriage so I should move out. I know he still loves me and wants me to try, I can't. I've done it too many times over the years! So as you can imagine it's hard for me to try and do anything at the moment. One minute he's ok, being helpful, helping me look for properties the next he's sulking. We had a row Saturday night. He punched me on the nose! I went ballistic, told him to get out. He wouldn't. He's very selfish always has been. So I hope you believe me when I say that I really do like you. I get agitated waiting to talk to you. You're always on my mind. Which is driving me potty?! It upset me reading your messages last night, you've done nothing wrong, It's my fault. I should have told u my circumstances. So if you would still like to meet me, we will. But I guess you won't want to know now. The thought of not talking to you makes me sad. The phone number I gave to you is to the phone I use for work, I leave it there. That's why I haven't phoned. Even though my hubby knows I don't love him and that I'll be gone hopefully soon, he doesn't like the idea of my having a new boyfriend. I suppose I can't blame him for that. I guess if the boot was on the other foot... We've spoken about meeting other people. He's just said that if I have a heart, I wouldn't do it while were still living under the same roof. So I've not wanted to, till now. I wasn't expecting to get on with u so well. Anyway, If he's around it's very hard to talk about feelings on chat. I guess I won't have to worry about that now. I didn't intentionally mean to lie to you, technically I'm not, we're not, together. I guess this is goodbye, I really hope not. It's up to you to if you still want to talk to me. Take care..........

Loren xxxxxxxx.

Joe sat back his coffee growing cold. Alarm bells rang in his head as he finished reading Loren Green's email. It was Mrs Loren Green in fact and not Miss. He had done it again. He had stumbled upon trouble and taken it with both hands and this time he had opened his heart and hoped to care. The message in itself was very repetitive but it shouted almost screamed at him for attention. Loren had at least been honest with him. Okay she had lied on chat that first time by saying she was single, but in a sense Joe figured that she was. He brushed away the warning signs and read the message over and over again imprinted the words on his mind. Loren repeatedly mentioned him as though he was always in her thoughts just like she was always in his. This had to be right.

Joe didn't have to wait long after reading the shocking email from Loren before she popped online. She was obviously anxious to explain herself to him face to face or at least camera to camera. So he accepted her invitation. He just stared at her not able to type anything at all. He looked at her on camera she was smiling as normal, but there seemed to be an uncertainty he could read in the way her lips were moving. She seemed anxious.

"You okay with me, Joe?" she typed breaking the silence.

"Just read your email" he told her. He was grateful that she had been the one to start the conversation off. He really didn't know what he was supposed to say to her. He found that he was really growing fond of his chats with Loren. He had been looking forward to eventually meeting her. Finding out she had a husband was a shock he hadn't been prepared for. He thought back to the time she twirled for him on the camera. There had been no children about, no husband. That's when it clicked. The husband had obviously taken their children on some kind of day out.

"So you still want to be friends? And no before you ask I do not share a bed with him. I sleep with Tim, my youngest."

"So is he there now?" Joe typed feeling anxious and ignoring her question completely.

"No he is in bed."

"Well yes. I'm still here. More fool me." Joe said trying hard to hide his anger.

"Good I'm glad. You're a lovely bloke Joe Hughes. Please don't be angry at me. I want you to understand how hard things are for me. I still want to meet you."

"I don't know what to say to you Loren, but I think you can already guess that I'm not going away just yet."

"We live like strangers, "she continued. "I just want to get somewhere nice. It was tolerable living here before I met you Joe but now it's terrible. He punched me in the nose the other night we had a blazing row. I told him I wanted him out. He refuses to leave. Says it's his house too."

"Are you okay?" Joe typed concerned and worried for this new woman that had entered his life. To think she was with someone that could hit someone with such beauty filled him with an anger he had never felt before. He felt the anger he had felt over her lies being pushed diverted to her husband. He wished he could do something to take her away from it all. Protect her somehow. There was nothing to do though he was no knight in shining armour. He lived in a caravan of all places outside his parent's house. He was in no position to help anyone.

"I will live. Bloody hurts though lol. But sooner or later I will sort myself out don't you worry about that one."

This was a story Joe would hear often. Hearing it for the first time Joe was saddened. He wanted to help Loren. He wanted to be there for her and look after her, to take her away from the awful sounding man that was her husband. A little voice spoke out in the back of his mind, there's always two sides to every story Joe, the voice said with grim certainty. Joe pushed his doubts away.

"So we still going to meet up for a lunch he asked her?"

"Yes. I'd like that a lot she said. "but I have another idea. Why don't you come to the hospital when you finish work? Meet me for a coffee?"

"What about lunch?" Joe typed feeling like she was fobbing him off for the first time.

"We can still do that too," she said, "and maybe go out for a night out. I just want to meet you and see you. It's lovely to see you on cam but I find I miss you when I'm not online.

"I miss you too," he typed and it was true. When he was online which seemed to be more and more lately he had a bitter taste in his mouth when Loren wasn't there. When he chatted to people, or more importantly to say when he messaged other women online he had become distant. He was just biding his time for when Loren would pop up and chat to him. He now knew it would be a lot more difficult than he thought.

"Look I have to go now hubby is waking up," she typed. "Can you promise me one thing Joe?"

"What?" His palms were sweaty as he typed. He felt as though something bad was about to pop through in her next message. How stupid he felt for a little thing like a typed few words to affect him so much.

"When we are online can we just talk as friends for now and not mention meeting up. Unless I let you know that the coast is clear. He doesn't mind me chatting to people online but I don't want any trouble at home. Always ask me to put my web camera on so you know it's me. Like I said he doesn't mind me chatting on line, but he can be quiet devious when he wants to be."

"Ok," he replied simply."

"Got to go nowwwwwwwwwww," she typed followed by a row of over ten 'x's for kisses. At that her status changed to offline and she was gone leaving Joe sitting at his screen feeling like he was losing something good. He wanted to impress her somehow. He felt he needed to prove his worth so that he could win the woman's heart.

Joe decided that if things between him, and the new woman in his life were ever to work out he would need to do something special. Joe loved his music. He knew well from the short time he had spent talking to Loren that music was a big part of her life too. He went online looking for concert tickets. He knew it was crazy, but he wanted to have something planned for the future. Joe just wanted to give them both something to look forward to, a goal if you will. So it was that Joe found himself looking on the online website for the Civic Hall in Wolverhampton. On browsing the various different bands that were playing he came across a name that reminded him of old times. About a year earlier Joe had taken his sister Shirley to a concert. Joe's sister never really got to go to things like concerts so it had been a real treat for her. At the time Joe had planned to take his wife. It was going to be just another attempt at saving their slowly shattering marriage. The artist in question had been Darren Hayes the lead singer in an Australian band called Savage

Garden. He had promised himself that if Darren Hayes were ever to play again he would have to get tickets as it had been one of the best live performances Joe had ever witnessed. It would be good to take a woman with him that wasn't related to him, he found himself thinking with great amusement. Someone he could kiss passionately the way Mr Hayes had done with one of his female fans near the end of the concert as he had sung to the crowd. So getting out his credit card Joe ordered two tickets thinking that even if Loren turned him down he would easily be able to find someone else to go with him.

After making himself a cup of coffee Joe just sat at the stool in the kitchen for a very long time. He could not believe what he had just done. He had ordered two tickets for Darren Hayes for a concert three months in the future. He had bought them with the idea of taking this new woman in his life, this beautiful creature that seemed to smile at his every word and laugh at his every dry witted comment. He did it without thinking but it felt right. For the first time in his life he seemed sure of himself. He wanted to get to know this woman a great deal. It wasn't about sex; this was nothing like before with the countless number of women he had met online over the past 3 months. No his time of internet slagging about was out of his system. She seemed both warm and caring, yet there was a sense of a free spirit about her that attracted Joe like no one else had. This was way beyond what he had felt for Katrina, Isobel hadn't even come close. It was sheer madness he had yet to even meet the woman. He had no way of knowing they would even get on. Yet something in the back of his mind seemed to sing him a lullaby. It was such a sweet song and he felt everything would be alright. This time he told himself things would work out. He had given Loren his number very quickly, but then that always his way. He never saw any harm in giving out his mobile number to anyone even if a few of the women he had met turned out to have deep psychological issues at the end of the day.   After all if someone he gave his number out to proved to be a bit dubious then all he needed to do was simply not answer his phone. It wasn't until much later he would realise that with this women it would never be that simple, nothing ever would for Loren was the biggest Pandora's box to ever walk into Joe's crazy world. Still as he stared at the screen having just filled in his credit card details to purchase the concert tickets he was happy. He knew without a shadow of a doubt that Loren would go with him, even though it was three months ahead and they had yet to meet. Still she seemed keen to meet up. Had it not been Loren after all that invited him to meet her at her place of work? The flirtatious nurse had given him directions of how to get to Hope Springs Hospital in Sutton Coldfield, directions he was sure he would need to clarify on his way there. Geography had never been Joe's strong point. He remembered when at school sitting the exam he had filled the entire exam paper out only to realise all the questions needed to be answered on a separate piece of paper. Needless to say Joe Hughes failed Geography with grand flair.

    The next day he was at his computer again. He was selling a large number of things on the auction website Ebay, and doing quite well for himself. Joe told himself that one day he would make a living off the auction website and stop working his nine to five job. He would buy books from second hand stores as well as computer games. Whenever he got the chance he would visit car boot sales picking anything he thought would do well online. I won't work for the man for ever he kept telling himself. What he meant by this was simply that he wouldn't always work for someone else. Joe wanted nothing more than to be his own boss. It was a dream he knew that, but sometimes dreams come true. He hoped Loren would come onto chat but after working on Ebay for several hours, taking photographs of the books, console games and other items he was selling, he decided to call it a night. He would go back to the caravan and read a Terry Pratchett novel. The wacky author's books always left Joe Hughes in high spirits. Smiling at how good his online selling was going he was just about to turn off his computer when Loren's name suddenly popped up. She had logged onto chat.

"Hiiiiiiiiiiiiiiiiiiiiiiiiiiiiiiiii" she typed holding he finger down on the 'I' key.

"Hellooooo" responded Joe with equal exaggeration.

"My partner in Crime…. Yes" she typed in response. "give me two minutes" she added.

"So what have you done when are the police going to arrest us?" Joe joked.

"lol," she replied meaning Laugh out loud in chat speak, "Don't go. I just have to check on dinner and the kids."

Joe thought the woman was amazing. Not only did she have a respectable job as a nurse in a maternity ward, but she seemed to cope very well with a horrific sounding home life. Four kids to bring up and a husband that seemed to be quite happy to sit around and let her look after him like some kind of waitress at his beck and call. Sure Loren had told Jack that they were living separate lives and that she wanted her hubby Adrian to leave. But Jack knew from the life lessons he had learned that things were never crystal clear. There were always two sides to every story and he knew that sooner or later he would find out both sides to this one too. Still he liked Loren. He liked her a great deal more than he thought possible for someone he had never met. He wouldn't rock the boat, not yet. He didn't want to blow his chances and finally finding happiness. That was strange though wasn't it even then? Here he was typing away to a woman who was essentially married. But then had he not been there himself? He knew what it was like to live in a world where your life seemed pointless as misery followed you at every step. Joe had gained his freedom. It had taken him five long years. Loren had told him on a previous occasion that she had finally snapped two years back when her mother had died. There seemed to be no love left in her marriage. Joe was certain of this for whenever he looked at Loren from their her webcam and seemed to bring her into his very home, he could see when her husband was nearby as her face seemed to contort each time into one filled with anger. Then when she looked at Joe she seemed to beam with a happy smile. She was so full of life. And while sometimes she didn't always turn her camera on for him she always insisted he turn his on for her so that she could see his face.

"Give me 2 minutes."

"Why?" he asked.

"Patience is a virtue." Loren typed back.

So Joe waited for what seemed like forever. Other people messaged him in chat but he did not respond. He was only interested in Loren. So he sat there patiently for what seemed like an eternity sitting watching his screen, ready for that flash at the bottom telling him she had sent him a new message. In reality it was only ten minutes before she came back as the clock on the bottom of his computer screen told him.

"Back," she typed.

"So I see," He smiled.

"You have a lovely smile Joe. So do you want to play a game?" she typed.

"What game would that be?" Joe enquired. "Eye spy? I can hardly see all the things in your house."

"lol" she typed giving the ever so usual internet response. She beamed at him with her lovely eyes. Joe had never seen a woman that seemed so alive. How odd it was that he should find such a person online after all the nutballs, and one night stands he had encountered. Surely this woman would become more than that. He sensed it very strongly and it made him have butterflies just thinking of when he might speak to her next.

More people messaged Joe. Little bars flashed at the bottom of the screen of his monitor. Joe closed each one. He only had eyes for Loren now. He was spellbound by her sarcastic charm. They were very much alike He felt as though he had found a kindred spirit in this woman he had met online. It was strange seeing as they had hardly spoken at all.

"So what's this game?"

"Checkers"

So they played what would eventually become their game. It was the most fun Joe had ever had online. No chats about getting into Loren's knickers. No requests for some one night stand meeting that would just be sex. It was nothing more than a fun game between two people that got on overwhelmingly well who had yet to actually meet. They talked about everything and anything finding out all they could about each other. Loren loved her music. They would often time in song's lyrics getting the other to guess the title of the song. Joe had never had this much fun chatting to anyone else online.

    Over the next few days they spoke even more on the phone when Loren was on duty as Hope Springs. They chatted online almost every night knowing that in a few days they would meet up and either they would get on or all the fuss would have been for nothing. Joe was nervous, but had an overwhelming feeling in his head that told him everything would work out just fine.

Joe sat on the bus that Loren had told him would take him to Hope Springs Hospital. His phone was clenched tightly in his hands. He didn't have a clue where he was going only that the bus would take him past the hospital. He also knew without a shadow of a doubt that he would be unable to resist calling her. Of course he had to didn't he? How else would he know where to get off? There will be a great big bloody sign that says Hope Springs, the little voice of reason at the back of his mind told him. Still that didn't matter to Joe he just wanted to hear the sweet sound of the woman he had met online a few weeks earlier. He sat nervously on the bus for a good twenty minutes. The bus moved slowly. Traffic was terrible and of course why shouldn't it have been. He had missed the first bus and waited another twenty minutes before the next one showed. He just hoped he wouldn't be too late. If he got there too late Loren would perhaps be in theatre or maybe would be unable to take a break. So as he sat watching unfamiliar scenery pass him by he was as nervous as a school boy about to kiss his sweet heart for the first time.

Eventually Joe could wait no longer. He went into his contact list on his phone scrolled down to Loren and dialled her number. The phone rang out, finally stopping after three maybe four rings.

"Hiya Joe. Where are you?" Loren asked him. She sounded as cheerful as ever. Joe would have gone on record to say she was the most carefree person he had ever spoken to. She never seemed to have a worry in the world despite her situation at home.

"I'm on my way to see you of course. Traffic is mad and I haven't a clue where I'm going." He told her.

"It's manic here," replied Loren, her voice as soft to Joe as ever. "I'll try and get a break when you get here. Won't get long but least we finally get to meet."

"I've just passed a pub called the horseshoe. Do you know it?" asked Joe. He felt like he was on some magical mystery tour with no idea where he was headed.

At that Loren laughed. It was a good well natured sound full of fun. "I have never heard of it in my life," came her reply with more laughter following. "Look Joe I really have to go. Give me a call when you reach a pub called the Old Boot. Hope Springs is just past there."

"Okay I will. Have to say I'm really nervous."

"Don't be I'm just me."

"Well I can't help it.

"You'll be fine," she replied before wishing him goodbye and hanging up, adding, "I will see you soon Joe Hughes."

Taking the phone from his ear Joe let his mobile rest in his hand upon his lap and kept an eye out as the bus continued its slow frustrating pace. He just wanted to get there to see her. It was a good fifteen minutes later when he was finally able to call Loren back as he passed the pub called the Old boot. She told him to get off the bus two stops after the bus and just as she said it he jumped up out of his seat running to the front of the bus. He could see the sign for Hope Springs clearly in the distance.

Arriving at Hope Springs Joe didn't have to wait long before his new found internet friend showed up with a warming beaming smile dressed in a baggy blue uniform pair of hospital scrubs with bloody shoes to top it all off. She looked radiant to Joe. She walked towards him like the happiest person to set foot on the planet. Loren looked more than pleased to see him, and completely at ease. Joe thought that rather strange for someone who had never met anyone off the internet before.

"Hope your journey wasn't too long." She beamed at him with a smile. She fished out a packet of cigarettes from her top pocket, they were royals and offered one too Joe as she lit one up for herself."

"I'm trying to quit," Joe told her taking the cigarette anyway. He couldn't get over how calm she was. He was as nervous as hell on meeting her. He couldn't believe how attracted to her he was. He wondered how she felt about him on finally seeing him in the flesh.

"One won't kill you," she laughed. The woman was so full of life.

"So what do you think now that you have met me in person?" Joe asked waiting for that eventual disappointment as she told him he wasn't what she had expected.

"You're just the same, Joe I don't like you for what you look like though. It's your personality that I'm attracted to you should know that, but seeing as you asked me why don't you let me know what you think was I worth the journey?"

"Yes you certainly are worth the magical mystery tour I have just taken. Your hair looks a bit lighter than it does on camera, He laughed, "but otherwise you're just what I expected, the same nutty woman I have been chatting and speaking to for the last few weeks. Only now you have blood on your shoes." Joe said smiling as he puffed away on the first cigarette he had had in several weeks. He would never be able to quit after that day. His life would change forever.

Finishing their cigarettes Loren led Joe to a small canteen inside the hospital. There were only about half a dozen round tables each with two or three chairs placed around them. So they sat down and chatted some more. Joe ordered them two teas as they talked about Joe's journey and Loren's difficult situation. At one point a woman came in with her young son needing to use the toilet that was situated at the far end of the canteen. She had a small blonde haired boy with her that looked about seven years old. She seemed a bit worried about leaving him in the canteen on his own.

"Don't worry I will watch him for you," Loren said smiling at the woman.

The woman thanked Loren for her kindness. It was obvious to Joe that seeing Loren in her uniform made the woman feel safe to leave her boy with someone she had never met. Absurd maybe, but Loren had a look about her; it was in her eyes, her smile. It was a look that could win over anyone. So the woman left her son with Loren for just a few moments so that she could use the toilet facilities. When she came out in what seemed a hurry it was only to be expected, Loren after all was a complete stranger. Still she thanked the nurse with the overpowering smile once more as she led her son out of the canteen.

"You seem to be the sort of person that wants to help everyone," Joe told her as they made their way back outside for one last cigarette before they bid each other farewell. He had enjoyed watching the way she was with the boy and his mother. How she helped out as thought it was second nature to her to do something for others, not herself. Joe would find out late that Loren was like that all the time, especially with strangers. When it would come later to people she cared about he would find it was another story, but it was early days, they had only just met.

"I do what I can," she told him, blushing.

"So you got here okay in the end then?"

"Thought I'd be late to be honest," he told her. "I didn't stop to think how bad traffic would be. Everyone was leaving work to get home and all that. I have never been to Sutton Coldfield before in my life."

"Well you got here in the end that's what counts." She smiled. "So I was worth it then?"

"Most definitely."

She laughed at his comment "well I'm just me," sorry I couldn't dress up for you in a sexier uniform."

"Not to worry," Joe told her as he finished his cigarette, stubbing it out on the floor.

"So bet you have met loads of women off the internet haven't you. Bit of a male slag really. God knows what you think of me with my hair all a mess and in these terrible clothes." She gave him a sly grin.

   "You know full well I have slept with more than a few women," Joe replied without any hint of offence in his voice. Not that he was offended. He had been honest with Loren from the start hoping she would accept him for who he was and not look at him too badly for his past. Of course she obviously didn't or why would she be standing with him now. Two people enjoying a few laughs as they met up briefly for the first time smoking cigarettes. They compared notes on reality versus the internet and agreed that they still liked each other and meeting up for lunch the following week would be great.

"I'm not easy," Loren told him just before she had to go. "I'm not like those tarts you have met on the internet, no sir. I'm as innocent as a nun."

"I never said you were," replied Joe and at that they bid each other farewell as Loren still had a long shift ahead of her. She told Joe how glad she was he had come out to see her. He left with a jump in his step glad things had gone so well knowing he would see her again soon, speak to her again too. It was only half an hour later and they were chatting about nothing and exchanging sarcastic comments as he made his way home on the bus. Sarcasm would prove to be another thing they had in common quite heavily and later on it would get them into many an argument and many a loving embrace. Joe didn't know that then, he only knew his first meeting with the woman he had come to miss with every passing minute had been just as warm in person as she was on his computer screen.

After that first meeting their online chats seemed to grow, as did the feelings Joe had for the woman he had met with the carefree smile and bloody shoes. He had almost quit smoking too.. Well that was out the window after accepting Loren's cigarette, not that he could blame her for his own lack of will power. Joe spent an increasing amount of time at his PC sitting on the high stool in his parent's kitchen. He kept himself busy with Ebay, only really wanting to see his screen flash at the bottom to tell him Loren had logged in. The next evening she was back, they chatted once again. At least from now on he would know where he stood if she went silent for a time or had to disappear.

"I just want to talk to you all the time." Loren typed, halfway through one of their many chats.

"That's how I feel except now I know why I couldn't." Joe typed back thinking back to that fateful email. Had he known from the start that she was married would he really have backed off or would he have carried on chatting regardless? Joe didn't have an answer to his question. What he did know was that he still wanted to talk to her now. "I just wish you had been honest from the start. That night when I went out with my friends from work all I could think about was how much you would have enjoyed it. I know how much you like your music. We would have had a great night dancing. Now I know things will be hard for a long time as you're a married woman. It just all seems wrong but I think I have fallen for you."

"Why have you fallen for me? I'm nothing special."

"I just want to sit with you in the real world and have a drink with you. You're very much like me," Joe typed his message in reply never feeling more able to be honest with anyone else in his life.

"Two peas in a pod" they both typed simultaneously followed by "snap"

It was uncanny how alike they were. Both their faces beamed with joy for the other to see. It was weird how they had both typed the same thing. It was like they were the same person. Soul mates are what they eventually came to call each other through text and online chat.

"Yes we are very much alike Joe. We are both bonkers."

"It takes a nutter to know one," Joe typed with an ever widening grin on his face.

"I can't wait to talk to you tomorrow. I'm in work at 7 lol so I hope I will wake up for work. "she typed laughing from her own side of cyber space while twirling her long wild hair with her fingertips.

"You had bloody better not sleep in" Joe replied Jokingly knowing full well regardless of what he said she would still call him anyway.

That next morning he nearly slept in. Joe would have been late for work if it hadn't been for Loren's call. As they talked he quickly got dressed. Pulling on his shirt and trousers, doing up his tie, as he held his mobile in his free hand as he spoke to Loren. He was glad she had called. It was then that they arranged to meet for lunch. She told him she would meet him later in the week on the Friday at one O'clock. He told her that he worked just of Colmore

Row. Loren agreed to meet him just by the big Church, and then she said they could spend time swapping mad stories and making fun of each other. Joe would look forward to it he told her as he finished getting dressed. He had no time to shower or wash, he was late. Still he had time to chat to Loren so that was all that mattered. Luckily Joe wasn't late and his morning had started well by him being woken by the woman that was slowly having a very heavy presence in his life.

When Joe got home that day he found Loren online again. She told him she had been waiting for him. She didn't stop only telling him she would be online later to play checkers after all her kids were in bed. So later that night just like many others in the future Joe sat at his PC doing pretty much nothing until the time at which Loren returned so that they could play checkers.

It didn't take long for the week to slip by. Time always seemed to go faster when he was talking to the new woman in his life. So eventually Friday was upon him. He was going to see her again.

So it was that they did indeed meet up again. Loren had arranged to meet Joe at one o'clock for lunch. They suggested going to a pub and getting a sandwich. That never actually happened, instead they went for a drink. They had two pints each in their hour together. It was their second meeting which was great as far as Joe was concerned, as the first time he had seen Loren which had been at the hospital; she was so busy that she could only really spare him ten minutes or so. This time they had a whole hour. It wasn't long true but it was better than nothing.

"You're a clever man Joe, she told him as they talked while smoking, drinking and laughing together in the small space of time they had.

"Thank you," Joe replied feeling himself blush. It was good to feel so at ease with someone. He had never felt that at ease with anyone. He told her about some of the past women he had met online. He told her all about a girl called Becky who had only been 19 years old and whom he had found out had more than likely had a boyfriend in Worcestershire where she lived. Joe had only seen Becky a few times but she had never been a one night thing. Like most of Joes relationships that lasted more than one night, or day, his time with Becky had proved more than troublesome as he explained to Loren in great detail.

Looks wise Becky had been perfect. She had been a very small girl, only a size 6 with an absolutely perfect figure. It was just that she was like most of Joe's previous relationships; rather emotional. She seemed keen to have children. She eventually confessed to seeing a psychiatrist and told Joe that her mom was dying. This in fact turned out to be a big untruth that became worse when the lie switched to Becky saying it was she that was in actual fact dying. This all led to a lot of anguish for Joe which he had gotten used to with women. Loren seemed happy with his honesty. She talked more about her children and how they were the centre of her world. She told him of her love for her job. Joe's job was basically just something that brought money in. He hadn't been happy in his job for years. It was then that Loren laughingly told him how she carried a knife, only for protection obviously she had laughed. She showed it to him with what Joe seemed to think was great pride.

"Well when I'm on night duty or a late I have to cross a large field in the dark to get home," she told him. They held hands across the table. It was strange to do that on only their second meeting. I guess it showed how even then they felt so comfortable together.

When their time was up Loren followed Joe to his place of work insisting she was actually coming in with him. She was winding him up. Joe didn't mind he loved the way they played off against each other. It was then feeling very confident that he pulled her close to him and kissed her lightly on the lips.

She returned his kiss gently with a look of surprise on her face. "not very shy now are you Joe," she laughed.

Joe simply responded by kissing her again this time letting his lips linger slightly longer than the first time. "It was great to see you again," he told her feeling like he was floating on air.

"Your lovely and nice Joe," she smiled. It came to be something she always said to him. In a way it would in time infuriate him as for the most part she was very unreadable at times and kept her emotions to herself. Her words sounded sweet to him at the time though. They parted then with Loren telling Joe that they would have to arrange a proper night out very soon as she could do with a bit of fun in her life

So they had met twice. Their online chats continuing, the phone conversations going on for as long as Loren could let them without getting herself into too much trouble at work. Joe found he was happy for the first time in what seemed like around six years. He had grown to hate himself for all the women he had slept with online. He had shared this comment with Loren several times. She just insisted to him each time that it didn't matter. Loren liked Joe for who he was, his personality, and the feeling was overwhelmingly mutual.

They played checkers then like they always seemed to do. It became their thing. It wasn't really the game either of them was interested in no matter how fun it was. They were more interested in each other. The game was just an excuse to chat not that they really needed one, though perhaps with Loren's husband always in the background perhaps she needed some small excuse for her continued chats to Joe. So they played checkers again, it was only one of many games they played over the coming months. Loren always seemed to turn the game off just as Joe was about to win. As time went by he even spoke to her kids, all of them, even the youngest who just typed out little characters at random onto chat that appeared on the screen. Joe warmed to them all and imagined a time when five children would all be laughing together, Loren's and his son Reece. Reece even did his little bit waving on cam on the weekends he spent with his dad, asking if he could talk to the little boy he could see on the computer screen. It was a great time. Sure when they met up it would always be difficult. A large part of their relationship was online. They would talk for hours. Then there were the times when Loren was at work. She never had any credit on her phone but she insisted Joe always text her as she said she loved reading his texts. Over time they eventually became more sexual in nature with them swapping fantasies with Joe buying credit for Loren's phone as he hated just texting her and not getting any response back. Whenever he knew she was at work and even when she wasn't he would proclaim his love of her through text sending her so many texts any other woman would have felt pressured. Loren didn't though, or at least she never told Joe she did. On the few occasions Joe didn't have half a dozen texts waiting for Loren to read when she got to Hope Springs and turned on her phone he could sense the sadness in her voice. She would ask him where her texts were and of course they would then come thick and fast.

"Hiya Joe," typed Loren one Saturday afternoon.

"Hello nutty woman," he typed back. He had only gotten in ten minutes ago. He had been to pick up Reece who was content to play on the Game cube his dad had gotten for him while his father was in the kitchen on the 'Puter' as he called it checking his emails.

"Is Reece there with you Tim wants to say hello," Loren typed. The cameras were both on as usual. Loren looked a picture. The sun was beaming in from her kitchen window lighting her up completely. Usually she would have her laptop in the living room, but today it seemed she was happy to chat in the kitchen. At least now when she disappeared to make a drink for one of the kids Joe would have her in his sights at all times. Joe thought that was good. It would be fun to see her being a mom.

"Yes. I'll go get him." Joe typed back. He called out to Reece beckoning him into the kitchen. Reece came with a down look upon his face. The frown being due to the displeasure at having to leave his games console for more than two minutes. He picked Reece up placing him on his lap and got him to give Loren and her son a wave.

"bloody camera keeps falling." Typed Loren as she disappeared from view the camera toppling to the kitchen floor. When she had steadied it back on top of her laptop she smiled.

"Aww he's so sweet." Typed Loren on seeing Reece. Both Loren and her Tim waved back with great gusto.

"hdihdodhdop." Typed Loren's son Tim.

"Hjdohjdodjdo." typed Reece in response.

"brb dinner." Typed Loren going over to the far end of the kitchen to check on some pots on the stove.

"How old is Reece again?" Loren typed when she returned.

"He is 4," Joe told her.

"Dinner time." She typed sighing. "I will let you get back to your time with Reece. Sorry I couldn't chat for longer, but kid's need feeding then they want me to play monopoly with them lol."

"It's been lovely seeing you again." Joe typed finding himself sitting there staring at her image on screen. He knew she was staring back.

"I have to go now but I will thrash you at checkers tonight"

So that night with Reece safely in bed they did indeed both log on. Joe had to wait about twenty minutes with Loren at one point popping on just to say she wouldn't be long only for her to still be ten minutes later than she said she would be. Joe was happy when she did finally sit down to play their little game and gave her no word of complaint.

"I'm going to beat you at checkers."

"Would be just my luck, how are things with u or cant u talk?" he asked her accepting her invitation to view cam just as she did his.

"Let's play," typed Loren. Her answer spoke for itself. Loren either didn't want to discuss her situation online, or more than likely couldn't. Joe never actually saw Adrian on cam but he could always tell when he was around.

"Ok," he typed back simply, "get ready to lose,"

"We've an audience today. My daughter Harriet is watching the game."

"You look quite smart today!" he complimented her as he accepted her invitation to play checkers and began what he hoped would be giving her a complete thrashing.

"lol……..me smart, my hairs up. That's all. Brb phone" Loren typed taking her go quickly before a phone appeared in against her ear.

"Want to do this later?" Joe asked.

"No it's Okay. Just give me one minute it's my auntie. She's 84." She gave Joe a little wave with her free hand.

"It's ok," typed Joe as he waved back smiling. She was a barmy woman he told himself. He was a barmy man. They were a right pair of crazies.

"Right" Loren typed as she hung up the phone.

"I do believe you wanted me to beat you in a game of checkers." Joe typed.

At that she began to play the game. She was getting increasingly better. Joe didn't think she would win though, and he knew full well that if she thought she would lose she would simply close the screen as usual.

"oops." Joe typed as he watched Loren move her pieces to his advantage.

"Come on stop time wasting." She told him as she watched Joe thinking over his next move.

"You know you will lose." He told her laughing into the camera

"Never."

"Sorry not in a winning mood." Joe typed five minutes later when Loren suddenly seemed to get the upper hand. Most of his checkers pieces had started to disappear from the onscreen virtual checkers board.

"You know I'm going to win." She told him adding, "take ur gooooooooooooooooooooooooooooooooooo." She was growing impatient. It was obvious to both of them she would win at any minute. Of course she knew why he was stalling for time. Loren would more than likely have to sort her kids out when the game finished. Joe hated to see her go.

"Stop playing with your hhaaaaaaaaiiiiiiiiiirrrrrrrrr. No actually carry on I like it," He typed back with equal exaggeration.

Five more minutes later Loren had won the game. She waved her hands in the air in triumph and her daughter Harriet hugged her from behind.

"Mom finally beat you," typed Harriet.

"She must have been practicing hard against you guys," Joe typed back in response.

"Just look into cam a min. you're nice," typed Loren her daughter having disappeared from view. "Smile for me, Joe."

Doing as she asked him he received a smile in return which made him feel something he hadn't felt in a while. He couldn't quite put his finger on it but something was happening between them and he had no intention of stopping it.

"I'm going to let you get some sleep now." She said blowing him a kiss from her side of cyber space.

"Thanks will think of you Goodbye xx," he typed returning the kiss.

"I'll be thinking of you too." At that she logged off.

So their chatting for that night ended, only for it to continue as though they had never parted the following evening. Their chats certainly were becoming a big part of both their lives. It seemed to Joe that they were kindred spirits so alike it was like something out of a movie.

"Good evening" typed Loren. "I'm always thinking about you Joe."

"And me you."

"Strange isn't." She was staring at him smiling straight into the camera as though waiting for his response. "We'll sort out on phone tomorrow about meeting ok" she told him blowing him a kiss.

"Can I ask you something?"

"Yes." She typed.

"Do you believe in the same way I do that we have a lot in common personality wise (I'm not talking about interests) but the type of people we are?"

"Yes." She nodded her head smiling at him.

"And do you think it would be a waste to throw that away."

"Yes I do." She nodded again

"Or do you meet people like me all the time?"

"No never met anyone like you." Loren confessed. "You're just like me. I love your personality."

"If had my own place I'd invite u to move in tomorrow. I'm just sorry I don't."

"You couldn't put up with me...lol" she said typed the abbreviation for laugh out loud. "We'd be barmy. Lol"

"I'd take your batteries out when you get too loud and put you back in your box till I can cope again." Joe Joked.

"What about when I'm being silly"

"It's what I want the silliness. The way you play with your hair. The way we constantly chat about everything."

"Did I tell you about that car advert I like." Loren typed.

"Which one?"

"The one that goes I see you baby."

"Yes." He replied vaguely remembering the advert showing in the cinema the last time he had been. It was for a car he couldn't quite remember. What he did remember was woman in a white skirt shaking her behind quite vigorously as she held onto a lamp post. It was actually quite funny, with the shock tactic very catchy. He had an idea that it had been released, going straight to the top of the charts.

"SHAKING UR ASSS." She finished.

"And you don't have a point do you?"

"I love that advert."

"And I bet you would look lovely SHAKING UR ASSS" He said with a smile.

"You want to play cowboys and Indians. lol"

"Please please can I be a horse. No sorry naughty thoughts. Forget that" he typed becoming quite amused at the racy turn the conversation had suddenly taken.

"So I can RIDE YOU finished it off for you." Loren typed. A wide grin had spread across her face. She threw her head back laughing hysterically. Of course Joe couldn't hear her he could only watch, but he could tell she was pretty amused by her own shocking comment. Still he had pretty much asked for it. As usual they had both been thinking the same thing.

"It didn't start that way in my head, but that's how it ended."

"That's what I like about you" Loren told him.

"I just didn't want to be a cowboy or Indian. One thing led to another lol. It's like if you're given two options like the choice of two doors to take. I'll dig a hole and tunnel underneath making a new option. You're the only person I have met that actually accepts my nutty side and enjoys it."

"What do you think when you're looking at me?" she asked.

"Most people laugh and get that I'm warm and kind but no one seems to get me like you do."

"We're two peas in a pod." They both typed.

"I know this is going to be hard for me but do u want me to hang in there? It's what I want, but I want to know if you want me to just think I found someone I can be silly with lol" Joe typed feeling very nervous.

"It would be a shame to give up on something that could be good."

"I'm not giving up." Joe was adamant about that.

"You had better not." She smiled.

"I just think I'd be terribly hurt if you gave up on me."

"I won't." She said, Joe almost thought he could see her blushing.

"What am I going to do with you eh?" Joe typed as he stared at her face on his screen. That smile was always there.

"Oooooooooooo let me think play pillow fights or even better food fights. Could make love to me, slowly." She typed.

"Don't go there it's something I think about far too much for someone I hardly know." Joe was shocked but amused by her words, also turned on just a little.

"Weren't expecting that were you, Joe? Best stick to jumping on the beds and pillow fighting."

"No lol that makes my mind think of something else" he joked.

"What's that?"

"Just things imaging things going up and down in steady motion getting faster and faster." He typed as they both laughed together.

"I see where that would lead. I think we both need to calm down," typed Loren.

"Maybe I should take a cold shower," he told her.

"Have a hot one and I will join you, Joe." She blew him a kiss from her side of the camera which he returned.

"Think it's time for my bed. And no more comments or I won't sleep."

"Ok night night Joe. Don't let the bed bugs bite. Xxxxxxxxxxxxxx"

"I hope to see you soon then."

"And yes I am really looking for a house. Bye xxxxxxxx" At that she was gone again. Joe felt alone. He hated it when the chats ended. He was almost addicted to them, had come to depend on them like his very life's breath. He turned off the computer deciding he would go to bed. He knew he wouldn't sleep when he got there, but he had no need to be at his PC. He seemed to only want to talk to Loren. As she had gone for the night he saw no reason to stay at his stool in the kitchen.

They spoke the following day, while Joe was on his lunch break Loren called up. Apparently she had only a few minutes, but had something very important she wanted to tell him. Loren agreed to come out for a drink with him on the Thursday night, that very Thursday night. Joe was over the moon they would have their first real proper date. They arranged to meet where they had the time she had met with him for lunch, outside the Church opposite Colmore Row. She told him she wouldn't be able to get there till six thirty. It was the best she could do as Adrian would get highly suspicious if she left too early. In the past when she had rarely gone out she wouldn't leave till around going on eight. Joe didn't argue he would just potter around town after finishing work at five, more than likely smoke half a dozen cigarettes while he waited, becoming a complete bag of nerves by the time he saw her. He could cope with that he told himself laughing. Still he didn't let her go just like that. He told her he had something important of his own to tell her revealing how he had bought concerts tickets for November, for them both to see Darren Hayes. Loren was over the moon, she told him she had only ever seen the Monkey's and Steps it would be great, she would be delighted to go with Joe. She saw no reason why they wouldn't still be getting on they had too much in common for anything to possibly go wrong. At that she was gone leaving Joe to return to work. He sat at his desk half trying to concentrate on his job with his thoughts drifting to Loren.

    Joe stood waiting by the church like Loren had asked. He was anxious; worried that she wouldn't show at all. The first time he had seen her it had been easier as he had gone to her, while the second time it had been during his lunch break so if she hadn't have shown up it wouldn't have mattered. This time was different he had finished work, changing into jeans and a clean shirt in the men's and now stood cigarette in hand waiting for what seemed far too long. He was early she wouldn't even be on time for another ten minutes.

    Of course she turned up and on time too. That's one thing Joe always knew with Loren in the future. No matter what happened she never let him down in regards to being where she said she would be, not once. Many a time she would insist to him that if she didn't show up it would be with a really good reason and for him not to worry. She had four kids not to mention a husband after all so things were never going to be clear cut. Still Joe was there waiting to take her out on their first real date.

On seeing her he felt so nervous. She beamed her usual carefree smile at him across the church park as she walked to greet him. She was wearing a pair of jeans and the same brown short sleeved top he had grown used to seeing her wear so many times before. She looked more than good, she looked great, but then to Joe Loren always did.

"I thought you were going to be late, "He told her as they great each other with a warm friendly hug.

"I nearly was," she replied with a mischievous grin. "I was in my local pub. The bar man wanted me to stay. Was waiting ages for a taxi. Had at least 3 double vodkas while I waited."

Joe could smell the alcohol on her. She was probably nervous about meeting him. Maybe more nervous than him, after all it was she who had the spouse this time around not him. She had told her husband she was just going out for a night with the girls from work. She had been adamant about it. The night before Joe knew Adrian had kicked up a fuss. He never showed himself on camera. He never walked past her laptop Joe always knew when he was around. Loren's face would change from that sweet loving innocent look full of happiness to a snarling grimace whenever he was around. He was never that good at lip reading but always knew when Loren was in an argument with her husband.

"So you didn't wait for the drinking to start until you met me," he joked as she took his hand.

"Noooo," Loren said, extending her words in life as she did online. "I love my drink," she laughed. "Come on find me a pub she added.

So they walked for a good ten minutes heading for Broad Street where most of Birmingham city centre's best bars lay. Joe asked her about her kids to which she replied, smiling all the while that they were all fine and she hoped Reece was doing fine too. Joe hoped Reece was doing fine and told her he was. He never really knew for sure though. The only contact he had with Reece was at the weekends. Isobel never called him to let him know how his son was doing. They rarely spoke since their break up. Joe just hoped the divorce would go smoothly. His name was still on the house, not to mention a whopping loan for sixteen thousand pounds that was their joint responsibility. Joe hoped that Isobel would see reason if he let her take his name of the house she would have his name taken off the loan. He just wanted a clean break. Joe shared all this with Loren as they made their way towards Broad Street. He did try and broach the subject of her husband and whether he had any suspicions about her night out seeing as she didn't really go out that much. He was met by a wall of silence that was coated with that same sweet smile and eyes that always seemed to sparkle with life.

The first bar they came to was the Manor House. It was a very old building and very spacious inside with a large and empty dance floor surrounded by very old fashioned décor. It was Tuesday night so Joe hadn't expected many people to be out, especially as it was only just after six thirty. There could not have been more than a dozen people in the large bar including the pair of them.

"So what will you have," Joe asked as they stood at the bar, the barmaid was an elderly looking black woman with a thin frame and just as thin spectacles.

"Just a lager for me, Joe," She told him smiling as she looked around at the almost deserted bar.

"Ok. I'd like a Jack Daniels and coke, no ice, and a pint of speckled hen lager. See something that's just like you," Joe joked "You speckled Hen." Joe had found humour was a good ice breaker in the past. What happened next made him shiver. He thought to himself not another psycho. She said she wasn't.

At what he thought had been a light hearted comment Loren slapped him lightly across the face, her hand moving as quick as an old west gunslinger's, She hadn't hit him hard, but still it was enough to shock him into silence. That was a first for Joe who had been called everything from chatterbox to gob all mighty by the people he had met over the years due to his inability to ever shut up. Well Loren had solved the problem with one slap. He was speechless. Things didn't seem to be going too well. He wanted to get them both seated as quickly as he could. A nice chat was what they needed. He didn't like the concerned look the thin black woman was giving them as she placed their drinks on the bar waiting for Joe to hand over the money.

"He knows just how far he can push me." Loren told the barmaid with the sound of laughter in her words

"She's mad," Joe laughed trying to act like he wasn't fazed. Know how far he could push her he thought. This was their first real date he certainly hadn't expected a slap so soon.

Paying for their drinks Joe found them a quiet place to sit, which to be honest could have been anywhere as the place looked almost deserted. A few people had already left since their arrival.

Joe offered her a cigarette and they both lit up. Loren moved closer to Joe so that her chair was at his side, smiling at him as she did and holding his hand in hers.

"Why do you like me so much?" she asked. Her hand moved over his knee as she stared into his eyes as if seeking the answer from within them.

"I don't know," he told her in the oh so quiet Manor House. He was nervous, shaking, he knew how close she was getting, knew what was coming next, least he thought he did. There was no music playing which was good it gave them a chance to talk.

"Give me your tongue, Joe," Her reply wasn't what he had expected.

Her words surprised him, but he wasn't about to argue. He had only kissed her once before. He had been waiting to do so again. She seemed more eager than him. There was a hunger in those wonderful eyes of hers. Moving his lips to hers he kissed her willingly slipping his tongue into her mouth. The kiss was amazing, at least to Joe. He had always been quite nervous about

French kissing due to being tongue tied at birth which basically meant until an operation at the age of ten he was unable to stick his tongue out very far. The fact that this woman had asked for his tongue and was enjoying it made him feel very at ease.

When Loren pulled away from him he was shaking, short of breath and felt in a world of his own, or rather their own. It was great to be with her. So romantic to just sit there and be able to kiss her, and yes they were very much alike.

"Wow!" He exclaimed when he finally got his breath back.

Loren just smiled at him.

"So how's your nose?" he asked concerned about what she had put in her email the week before.

"Bloody hurts." She replied rubbing it instinctively. At that she laughed.

"I really don't get it. You seem like such a strong willed dominant woman. Can't see how you could possibly put up with any man telling you what to do let alone hitting you."

"I know. I know." She repeated herself smiling all the while. The smile was infectious and Joe couldn't help return it. "I guess because I have lived with him since I was sixteen I kind of, I don't know put up with him. He is probably the only person that I let get away with it.

Certainly where the kids are concerned I am the boss in the house. They are all scared of me." She laughed again.

"Do you think it will ever change Joe asked staring into her eyes. He still couldn't get over how attractive she was. He just didn't she why such a beautiful woman would be sitting in a bar with him. Sure he had met beautiful woman before. He had bedded many, but he hadn't really dated anyone all that much. Joe had basically either got involved in bad relationships or slept around keeping his emotions firmly in check. It was proving difficult to do with Loren.

"I don't know. I think after my mom passed away with cancer two years back then that kind of made me harder. I can be a real bitch to Adrian sometimes. He won't come near me when I've had a drink," she smiled squeezing Joe's hand lightly. "Took a knife to him once he got me so angry he had thrown a plate at my head." With her free hand she pointed to a scar just above her left eyebrow. "My mom used to love her music. Especially all the old stuff. Her favourite song was Baby love by the Supremes.

It was then that something wonderful happened something Joe always told Loren in the future that he believed was a message a blessing from her mother. Call it fate call it what you will, at that moment the quiet bar burst into song as Baby Love suddenly played through hidden speakers somewhere high in the rafters of the bar.

Loren went to speak again to carry on talking about her mother.

Joe hushed her. "No. Don't speak let's just sit her and listen to it."

"This is so weird," she replied a look of amazement spreading across her face"

"Maybe it's your mother's way of saying it's OK and that she approves of me."

They listened to the song in silence letting it play all the way through. The only other sound was the tapping of their shoes to the music.

They left the Manor House ten minutes and another drink later both shaking their heads in wonder. Perhaps it was fate that had brought them together. The next bar they went to was known as the Aussie bar.

Loren insisted with great glee that Joe was paying. Joe wasn't exactly used to this but had asked Lauren out so didn't complain. He was used to his women paying their own way and was unaccustomed to paying the whole way.

Taking their drinks Loren led them to some steps at the far end of the bar. The place wasn't exactly packed but it was definitely a hell of a lot busier than the last bar they had been to. As soon as Joe had sat on the steps she sat astride him and began to kiss him passionately.

"You want to fuck me don't you Joe." She whispered to him repeatedly in between kisses.

Joe didn't know how to reply. He just kissed her back as passionately as he could his breath seeming to disappear from him. He wasn't used to this side of her but he wasn't complaining. The Loren he had been chatting to online always seemed so shy and there had never really been any hint of anything sexual between them even though they did get on extremely well. Still he did want her and he told he so, he also let her know he knew nothing would happen.

"No because I'm not easy she told him. Not like those slags you have met before," she laughed as she kissed him grinding her hips upon his groin thrusting herself upon him teasingly. The next thing Joe knew she had raised her top and he was sucking at her breasts. It was shocking but a turn on at the same time. What was he supposed to do when they were shoved demandingly in his face? He was only male after all. What guy would say no to such an invitation from such a great looking woman when she was moving herself in such a manner that made him so hard he couldn't believe it? On top of that he was shaking. He had never been like this with any other woman. He had always felt totally in control. Not this time. Loren was showing him she had a very wild side. Joe would do his best that night to prove he could handle it.

It was then just as things may have gone further, and in a crowded bar that would have been very bad for them both in the morning under a sober mind, that she stood up tucking her breasts away. She strode out of the bar her drink in her hand crossing the road, heedless of the traffic, to Reflex an eighties bar that was supposed to have a karaoke on that night.

Joe could do nothing but follow after her with his own drink; a pint of lager in his hand.

Of course as was obviously the case they never got into Reflex they were refused entry on account of them carrying drinks from another bar.

"You have obviously both had too much to drink," a large burly black suited doorman told them. "There is no way you're getting in here."

After an argument with the doorman that included Loren's insistence that she spoke to the management. When even the manager of Reflex refused her entry Loren had to admit defeat. Joe dragged her away keeping completely calm only for her to find something else that interested her. Just outside Reflex she spotted a paramedic astride a motorcycle. Glass in hand she began to have a casual chat as the paramedic did his best to tell her of the evils of booze, and how it was actually illegal to drink in certain parts of Birmingham out in the open such as the place Loren stood at that very moment. Joe just watched on at that point with amusement. He was happy, happier than he could ever remember being in a long time. It was good being out with Loren. The woman was a free spirit. He wondered what life would be like with her in the future if they ever had one, and found it strange that he would have such a notion after only knowing her for such a short space of time. They eventually left Broad Street behind. Joe coaxed Loren away from the argument that seemed would have no end telling her he knew of a quiet pub that also had karaoke where they could sing and drink to their hearts content.

Loren ran on taking her shoes off as she did and Joe followed behind her. Eventually she had to slow down and put her shoes back on, but by then they were both laughing so hard neither of them could manage more than a slow walk.

"You're a mad mad woman Loren Green," He told her.

"I'm just little old me," she replied.

They did indeed go to another bar that had a karaoke that night. They sang as Joe said they would to their hearts content, kissing as others sang and drinking with a real happiness between them. The first time Loren got up to sing she had to sing Like a Virgin by Madonna. Joe found her to have a wonderful voice. It helped no end when he turned her microphone on when she started singing. This she thanked him for with a kiss. They drank loads. They were both so enraptured with each other Joe didn't want the night to end.

Occasionally Loren would again tell Joe how she knew he wanted to fuck her but no way would he she wasn't like the slags he had been out with before. Her language shocked him, turned him on made him feel dizzy, and yet he was really at ease. Joe was having one of the best nights of his life and hoped Loren was too. There were several times when the drink spilled to the floor Loren along with it. Joe simply picked her up gently and got her a fresh drink. After singing several songs together the night drew to what had to be an eventual close.

Walking to New Street Station they made their way to the Taxi rank after a brief argument with a big issue seller who was obviously going for the seller of the year award what with him still trying to do business at such a late hour. Joe made a sarcastic comment that he had only bought twenty copies that day which only seemed to make the homeless man try harder. It wasn't until the police intervened that the homeless man wandered off. Joe was glad to see the back of him but a little dismayed when the police asked

Loren if she was okay, as if to say is this man, Joe, bothering you?

They sat beside the taxi rank for half an hour. Loren seemed so sad at the thought of going home.

"Why me Joe? Why me?" she said looking into his eyes with sorrow. "Why'd you like me so much?"

"I don't just like you, Loren, that's the thing. I can't explain it but my feelings are so much stronger than that.

"What?" she laughed seeming obviously shocked by his words. "You can't possibly love me. You hardly know me."

"I know it's strange isn't it. I do love you though Loren." He confessed. "I know its sudden and strange but the one thing I'm certain of is that I've fallen in love with you."

"You can't have," she said denying his words. "I just wanted a fun night out with someone I like and who likes me."

"I'm just telling you how I feel. I can't help it." Joe was getting emotional he could feel the tears in his eyes and had to fight hard to keep them back. He hadn't a clue what was coming over him.

A beep from Loren's phone interrupted them. It was a text from Adrian. Joe gazed at the phone as she read the message. It basically said that he hoped she was okay and that he loved her very much. Putting her phone back into her hand she looked up at Joe. "I have to go," she told him standing up. "My kids will be worried sick."

"He just texted you," He told her. "I read what it said."

"Well what am I supposed to do Joe not go home? You're a lovely guy you're just like me. I don't know what's going on."

"I can't help how I feel. You think I wanted to fall in love just like that? This isn't easy for me. I've kept my self closed off from women for so long after Isobel then you come along."

"There must have been other girls."

"None like you. You seem to get me. I am able to be me with you." Whenever Joe had met other women he had always tried to be what they wanted him, just like had with Isobel, with Loren he felt like he could be himself completely.

"I wish I could stay with you Joe, Pack up and leave, tell my husband I have met someone else. I can't though I have to go. My kid's will be waiting up."

Joe didn't argue with her. He even gave her the taxi fare home. He knew that she was going to have to return home to her husband sooner or later. He wished he hadn't seen that text though. If he had been strong enough emotionally he wouldn't have let them sit and talk for so long. He would have gotten her in a taxi sooner. He hadn't though. Their wild night was finally over. It had been one of the most fun nights out Joe had ever had. He felt completely at ease with Loren as though for the first time in years he was able to be himself.

Loren got into the taxi beaming him that same smile that always seemed so at home upon her face. "I'll call you at some point tomorrow. I'm on a late shift," she told him.

"Ok. Goodnight, Loren," he told her pulling her to him one last time and stealing himself one final kiss.

He watched her vanish from his eyes in the taxi before stepping into one of his own, heading for home. His head in a spin, through alcohol true, but also for the way the night had made him fall for what he realised was in love for the very first time.

Joe had work the next day. His hangover was barely tolerable. Loren could certainly put the drink away. He could barely remember how much they had drunk that night. So he sat at his desk happy, despite the pounding in his head that was accompanied by a weak nauseous feeling in his stomach. He quickly overcame that at lunchtime filling his belly with a few burgers from a burger stand in Birmingham City Centre. He scoffed them down and was glad when the feeling in his stomach subsided. He hadn't had any breakfast that morning. He rarely did. Nearly late for work he had only just managed to catch the bus into town. Now with the day half over he knew Loren would be back at work soon. She would probably text him to tell him what a great night she had with him. By then Joe would be back at work. Shortly after lunch at around two thirty Joe did indeed get a text which he read at his desk.

In his job there was a strict policy about mobile phones. They were supposed to be switched off at all times. Anyone caught could be sent home on the spot. The way Joe's head still pounded he would have welcomed the idea of going home.

The text wasn't what he had expected it read :

Joe I had a lovely night last night but really can't do this. It was fun, but I want a quiet life and things are too complicated at the moment. I hope we can still be friends and chat online.

At that Joe didn't know what to do. All he could text back was: Don't do this Loren we are good together. For the rest of the afternoon Joe was incredibly anxious, he had to speak to her. The idea that he had to wait several hours till five to be able to call her was unbearable. He wanted to make her see reason. He didn't want Loren of all people to become just another one night thing.

As soon as he left work he dialled Loren's number. She picked up straight away. Joe had feared she would be in theatre or busy with something else as had sometimes been the case in the weeks since they had started chatting on the phone.

"Hiya." Loren's voice sounded tired.

"What's going on?" Joe asked her finding his voice rising.

"I'm just not ready for this. You're a lovely man Joe. I don't want to mess you around I just want to be able to sort my life out and get my own place. I had a wonderful time last night. I think I got a bit carried away but it was a fun night.

"Yes it was and you were certainly very different from the last few times I have seen you, but all in all I think it went well."

"Yes it did, and as I said I had a lovely time. Just think I drank a bit too much."

"There's nothing wrong with having a few drinks," Joe protested adding, "I loved seeing your wild side it was nice to know you were so interested in me. You do like me I know it so why end things when they are just started? I don't want to be nothing more than a one night thing with me and you. I don't want to be just a bit of fun for a married woman."

"It's not like that at all," It was Loren's turn to sound angry. It was only fair of course Joe wasn't exactly speaking to her as calmly as he normally would. "I just don't want any complications in my life."

"Come on Loren me and you are great together and look what happened with that song. It has to be fate I don't believe in coincidence. "Joe had never spoken a truer word in his life. They had both felt that magical moment as clear as day that night.

"I know. Joe your right."

"So don't throw it away just yet give us time to grow," he protested. "Let's just carry on the way we are, talking online, and on the on the phone. I won't pressure you I know you want to leave your hubby soon. Just meet me when you can and I will be happy with that."

"Okay Joe," she conceded letting him win that round. She sounded tired. Not surprising seeing as how late they had been out the night before. She would have had to have been up early that next morning to take her four kids to school. The woman must have been shattered. "Look I have to go now," she told him adding, "But try calling back every half hour or so and I will talk to you when I can. Let's just keep it light though."

"That's fine," he told her lying and at that she hung up. He didn't like the way things had gone. All he could do was hope things got better. Too much had happened that night for him to just walk away.

So that night Joe did his best to keep things light as she had asked him. They talked when she could. Joe was happy. He thought for sure he had blown things before they had even begun. He went home that night and did some work on Ebay. Joe was addicted to selling things on Ebay. Sometimes he had good days sometimes bad. He loved waiting for the promotional days which basically meant he could list hundreds of items, for the most part comic books, for free. In between working on Ebay he would speak to Loren from time to time. They talked about the night out and Joe was pleased they had sorted things out. It turned out she had just been a bit embarrassed by her behaviour.

"But that's me," she told him. "It's good to know I can be myself around you."

Joe felt the same way. So for weeks things went on as normal. They talked on the phone for three days a week whenever they could. They talked online playing checkers most nights. The thing was things didn't seem to be getting any better after a time with the date of the concert growing closer and closer Loren had done nothing to change her situation. Joe found it hard to stick to his word and not tell her how much he wanted her to sort herself out.

Eventually they met up again for lunch despite Loren saying she didn't want to talk about things. She just wanted to see him again. Joe still asked her when she would leave. She had told him she wanted to be gone by Christmas. When they sat drinking again during Joe's lunch hour she conceded to him that leaving before Christmas would be impossible. She would need all the money she could get to pay for presents for the kids and Adrian had a gambling problem that meant he often dipped into their joint account spending all the money she had earned in a month on bets that sometimes paid off, but more often than not meant he had to borrow money off his family.

When Joe kissed her he didn't feel like he received anything back, not this time. It was like she was deliberately pushing him away. When his lunch hour was eventually up she simply hugged him and bid him farewell. He told her as he always did, whether it was online or off that he loved her. He was crazy about her. All he got was her usual response of I know you do.

It was as though after all that time chatting she was keeping her guard up so that she wouldn't get hurt. In the process Joe knew that it would only be him that would suffer. He would still get the odd call every now and then as Loren got a break she would call him from the hospital payphone. She was missing him she confessed, but she just couldn't go out with him. She asked him to be patient telling him that if he loved her as he said he did he would do that for her, but that he had to understand that it would be his decision. Joe simply told her there was no decision to be made. So it went on for over a month. They chatted on the phone whenever they got the chance. Things in a way went back to normal. Loren would pop online every other night, not as often as she used to but when she did come on she never seemed to want to leave. They would spend minutes just staring back at each other over cyber space. Checkers became there excuse to just sit and watch each other. As time went on Joe became frustrated with Loren. She hadn't made any progress in finding a place to leave and seemed happy for Joe to be on the phone to her at a moment's notice. Their conversations started to turn into arguments with Joe telling her she needed to move out, or throw Adrian out. Why she put up with a man that didn't work and gambled away the money she worked hard to earn he couldn't figure out and kept telling her each time he spoke to her. Their chats would always start in a fun manner ending with them both rowing over the fact Loren never seemed to be making any progress

Weeks went by without them meeting up again. Then one evening a he travelled home on the train he got a call from Loren. Then she delivered the hammer blow that appeared to end it all. It was then that Loren stated without question that things just couldn't go on. She felt too pressured by Joe to leave Adrian. She had no way of leaving before Christmas. She told Joe how she didn't want to hurt him so was just being honest as it would be better in the long run for the both of them if they just parted. Joe loved her she knew that and she was sorry he had fallen for her. She told him she felt too pressured by him and that she didn't want to see him again. She couldn't handle their relationship and only wanted to be friends. Hadn't she said the same thing just after their first night out?   What he feared would be their last. He tried desperately to change her mind but nothing worked

"I don't want to mess you about Joe. I'm just telling you how I feel. You love me but I can't love you back. My life's too complicated right now and all I need is a good friend. Why can't you just do that for me if you love me?"

She didn't love him it was as simple as that. Loren didn't want to be with anyone she needed time, space to sort out her life. She liked Joe a lot but she couldn't see how they could keep in touch any longer. She knew Joe wanted her to come out with him. She told him that it was unfair of her to keep talking to him, they had to break off all contact completely and not speak again. The only hope she would offer him was that maybe one day in the future if they both were single then maybe they could go out on a proper date together. Joe told her that was highly unlikely if she never left her husband. He fought back tears for as long as he could. Joe tried his best to reason with Loren for what was over an hour. He left the train station at Cotteridge walking through the park tears streaming down his burning cheeks as he told her not to hurt him, to still chat to him, there was no need for her actions. You're just being silly he tried telling her. There was no point him arguing with her. Loren's mind was firmly made up. She just couldn't cope with seeing him anymore no matter how much it hurt him he had to just get on with it. Maybe in time she would sort herself out. He got home and drank himself into oblivion that night crashing out on the bed in the caravan wearier than he had felt in a long time. Things always seemed so good between him and Loren. They still were as far as he was concerned. Perhaps it would do her good to have some space from him.

So he let her get on with her life. They didn't speak online after that for a while. They didn't talk on the phone. Joe concentrated on the weekends with Reece. In the week he buried himself in his work laughing with his work mates as if nothing in his life had changed. He went back to talking to people online. He had no intention of meeting anyone but it was nice to get back into wasting time with people talking about nothing. It just wasn't the same though. He didn't play checkers with anyone but Loren that had been their game.

He called up his friend Amanda telling her what had happened. By that time he had drunk half a large bottle of vodka. In his frustrated he was hitting the walls of the caravan with his fists so hard that his knuckles bled and the wood began to chip.

"You need to calm down. Get yourself some sleep, Joe. No woman is worth this. I should know I am one of them after all. She is obviously very confused. You can't do anything about it just let it go."

"I love her!" He found himself screaming down the phone several times before eventually calming down.

"Well you won't be good to anyone like this Joe. Especially not your son and he is the most important person in your life. She is married Joe face it. She won't leave. And if she does it will be in her own time. You can't force this."

"I didn't," he told her, tears streaming down his face. "I did everything she asked of me at every time."

"You need to let it go. Come on you have only just come out of a long marriage yourself. You slept with all those women. You will find someone else."

"I don't want to go back to being a male slag," he retorted. "I want more than that. I thought that's' what I had found."

"Look I hate to be blunt, Joe but it looks like you haven't found anything but trouble. Just do me a favour and get some sleep. Get yourself sorted then when you are feeling up to it pop over and we can have a drink together. Moan about our problems over a good meal.

"Okay you win," he told her. "I'll go to sleep."

"Good idea Joe, Good night."

"Night," he replied hanging up. He finished of the rest of the vodka before he did go to sleep, he cried himself to sleep and passed out, waking in the early hours of the morning with another hang over from hell. Creeping quietly into the house he drank two pints of water, before taking a third glass back to the caravan with him. He hoped that by the time he woke again ready for work his head would stop spinning. Luckily for Joe it did. So at least that was one less thing to worry about, not that it made him feel any better about the way things had ended between him and Loren.

The next morning Joe woke up not knowing what to do. He went to work almost hypnotized by the loss he felt. He had never met anyone so like himself. He just wanted to be able to talk to Loren. He thought he had found the woman of his dreams and it had all come crashing down. Joe was usually the joker at work. If any seedy comment or sarcastic remark was to be made Joe would be known as the one to do it. People always watched what they said around Joe knowing full well he would have a sly comment or two ready at a moment's notice. It was one of the things Joe prided himself on. He had a very quick, often dry wit. It had always helped him with the ladies. It had been part of what Loren had liked about him too. If only she could have seen reason. Her marriage was over and they always enjoyed each other's company. A week went by with no word from Loren at all. There were no phone calls, no online chats. It had all stopped. He knew it must have been hard for her but he just wished she could see that he wasn't coping without her, maybe then she would call him, try to work things out. She always said they had too much in common to throw it away. He had put his life on hold in a way. He had accepted that she had a husband not letting that stop his feelings grow. After another week went by Joe tried his best to get back to his normal jovial self at work. It was hard for him. His comments would often offend his work mates rather than make them laugh, but he quickly noticed, apologizing to the people he upset. So that was it. His relationship with Loren had ended before it had really been given a chance, at least in Joe's mind that's what had happened.

So few weeks later with no contact at all from Loren Joe arranged to meet up with his friend Amanda, the self-proclaimed Wicca. Joe always jokingly told everyone she was his friend the witch. In reality for Amanda being a Wicca just meant that she had a different viewpoint on life. He had Reece that weekend but took him around to Amanda's so that they could watch a DVD. Reece played with Amanda's son Toby upstairs on his PlayStation while the two of them discussed their relationship problems. In many ways they were similar. They were after all both seeing married people, both doing what they shouldn't.

Joe did his best to talk to Amanda about her relationship and listen when needed and she did likewise. They both seemed to be in the same boat, in relationships doomed to fail.

They made cocktails as Amanda cooked a large meal of chicken tortilla's with a side order of everything. There was fresh salad, potato wedges, rice, not to mention many various dips such as barbeque sauce and the very popular choice; mayonnaise. Whenever Amanda invited Joe round she always cooked enough to feed an army. She told him that it was the Scottish in her blood.

"Us Scots are the best hosts in the world," she would often tell him, or "It's good that you can feel so comfortable here that you can pass out on my sofa." This second remark was usually made after he had woken up late at night when he was supposed to have been watching some movie or another with his friend.

Of course by the time the DVD was put on, some comedy movie Joe had picked up from the rental shop starring Jack Nicholson and Diane Keaton, he was ready to do what he always did which was fall asleep. They had both drank a lot that night though Amanda seemed to always handle it better the night of the booze. The day after would be when his friend would pay the price. Amanda would wake up late only to spend the rest of her day moaning that she would never drink again. So he lay on Amanda's sofa as he had done before, drifting to sleep with thoughts of relationship pushed quietly out of his head by the effects of the alcohol in his body. Reece had fallen asleep a good few hours before in Toby's room. Joe had made sure his son was well covered, kissing him goodnight before continuing his drinking that led to his eventual passed out status on the sofa.

When Joe did wake from his slumber he found Amanda surfing the web on her laptop.

"You were snoring again," she laughed.

Joe put his head back down on the pillow, falling quickly back to sleep on the sofa. Tomorrow he would take Reece to the cinema to watch a bizarrely titled computer animated children's movie entitled Boo, Zeno and the Snorks. Moments later he was fast asleep.

The next morning he woke up Reece. Carrying him downstairs into Amanda's kitchen as quietly as he could he made his son a small breakfast that consisted of toast with some orange Juice he found in Amanda's fridge. They had all slept in past eleven. Amanda was still fast asleep while her son had most likely gone off with his mates to the local skate boarding park. After they had washed and changed they left quietly leaving Amanda to sleep off her hangover in peace. There was a cinema just five minute walk from Amanda's home in Rubery where Joe planned to take Reece. There they got a large bag of pic n mix sweets and set about watching the strangely titled; BOO ZENO THE SNORKS.

The computer generated kiddies movie was quite bizarre telling a tale of a cartoon within a cartoon with the lead title character Boo, as well as his friend, and enemies the Snorks finding them in a quest in the real world. It didn't do anything to hold Joe's attention, but Reece seemed to love every minute of it. Halfway through Joe received a text from Loren. It read:

I know your probably hate me now. I've been a complete prat. I really miss you Joe.

He was shaking. He hated her for that text. He was trying his best to get over her to get on with his life. It had been her that had pushed him away again. All Joe wanted to do was enjoy the film with his son. Still his phone didn't have much battery power left in it so he wouldn't be able to risk calling her at any rate. So he sat watching the rest of the movie with Reece with his hateful thoughts slowly fading as hope spread in his mind of some kind of future with Loren. Maybe she had seen sense this time. How many times had he thought that before, or would he do again in the future he wondered no longer able to concentrate on the movie at all.

When the film ended Joe took Reece out of the cinema leading him slowly to the bus stop holding his hand as they went.

"Have you had a good day?"

"Yes, but I'm sad now." Reece told him.

"Why?" Joe smiled looking down at his son.

"I'll miss you when you're gone."

"You will see me again next week," he promised, ruffling his son's hair playfully.

They didn't have to wait long for the bus. It was the first of two they would have to catch. This one would take them into town while the next would take them to Stechford. Once on the bus Joe decided to text Loren: can't really talk now. I don't hate you, but the battery is nearly dead on my phone. Love Joe.

Joe didn't know what else to put. He hadn't ever expected to hear from her again. As far as he had been concerned it was over and it was something he was slowly coming to terms with.

That evening with Reece safely back at his mother's Joe sat in the caravan pondering on whether he should give Loren a call. He didn't have a clue what to say to her, but was glad to have the space to think, not being able to call her what with his phone having died on his way to take Reece home. His mobile phone was fully charged now though, his finger itching to press the button that would bring Loren's voice to his ear once more. He decided instead to make himself something to eat. He certainly needed a good meal. He hadn't fixed himself any breakfast that morning, just Reece, so the only thing he had eaten was his share of the sweets he had bought his son at the cinema. No, Loren could wait. He figured she was working a late shift which meant she would be at Hope Springs until nine that evening. It was only just a few minutes past six. She could wait for him for a while, and if she really wanted them to get back together she would call him.

Why would she, a little voice in his head whispered softly, she thinks your phone is dead.

Joe cooked himself two steak and kidney pies he found in the freezer with some chips and baked beans. He wasn't really all that hungry, but forced himself to finish most of it. He left a few scraps of beans. Other than that the plate was clean.

With his stomach full to bursting he decided he had waited long enough. Joe took his mobile off charge, lay down on the bed in the caravan; the dirty plate discarded to the floor, and called Loren.

"Hello Joe. I didn't think you would call," she said answering immediately.

"I have only just got back from taking Reece home," he lied.

"You probably hate me now don't you?"

"NO I love you like the prat I am," Joe told her.

"I just realised after not hearing from you for so long how much I really care about you. I promise this time will be different. I know it will take a long time for me to get myself sorted. It won't be before Christmas because of the kids, but I hope you can hang in there."

"I don't have a choice," Joe laughed. "I'm in love with you. You're a barmy woman Loren Green. We are like two peas in a pod."

"I know. I've been a fool. It's taken me this time away from you to realise how much I care. I'm really falling for you. I admit I put my guard up with you, but I'm slowly lowering it. I didn't expect to feel like this about anyone. I guess it just scares me."

"Well for what it's worth I could never hate you."

So they began talking again from that night, both on the phone, as well as online. Adrian still had no idea what was going on. Joe didn't feel bad because as far as he was concerned from what Loren told him their marriage had been dead for years. It was inevitable that they would meet up again. Loren had finally admitted that yes she did care a great deal for him. She was as she put in one text falling in love with him, and could do nothing to stop it after bottling her feelings up for so long. Joe simply thought it was about time. He had never understood why the woman always seemed to have her guard up in regards to her feelings for him.

Things got better for Joe at work. He started to enjoy his job again. Without the constant worry over how Loren felt, or what she was doing he felt able to get back to normal. Their chatting became less aggravated with Loren seeming to listen to him more, and take on the things he was saying. She admitted he was right. It was obvious to them both that after Christmas she would have to move out. Joe even offered to help her financially as best he could. Loren told him she wouldn't ever take his money. Joe simply said that if things got too bad for her at home then there may not be an alternative. She really couldn't afford to move out without getting a loan of some kind. With Loren being black listed, and in severe debt it didn't look like any bank would touch her. She did say she could ask her father, but that seemed like a dead end to Joe too as Loren kept her marriage troubles to herself, and rarely discussed anything with her family about all Adrian had put her through.

Still, with them back talking properly they laughed just like before. They played checkers as they had done so many times in the past. Joe even helped out Loren's kids with their homework from time to time. When she wasn't available to play checkers, or had to cook the family meal one of the children would pop on and try to beat Joe at checkers. Things seemed to have moved forward. He was becoming a part of the families life. Adrian not knowing how far Joe's relationship had actually gone with his wife told Loren he liked Joe, that he was a good friend to her and that if she ever did meet someone he hoped it would be someone like Joe.

They arranged to meet up again. Loren had asked Joe to come and see her when she was working at the charity shop one Thursday lunch time. Joe had booked the day off work with Loren insisting that as it was just voluntary work she could spend a few hours with him.

Waiting in the Yentob pub in Wylde Green like she had asked him to Joe kept checking the time on his watch, kept staring out the window to see her approach. He had ordered her a large glass of white wine as she had told him to by text and got himself just a coke. He wanted to be able to talk to her; he didn't want drink getting in his way. Things had been very bad between them of late. After that time on the train when she had told him she wanted nothing more to do with him relationship wise he had found it hard to cope, then there was the night he had gone almost crazy after he had heard nothing from her and he called her at home. He had only had her home mobile number a few weeks at that time and everything just spiralled out of control.

When she finally arrived Joe checked his hands. He was shaking. He couldn't understand it. Whenever he was with her he seemed to get the shakes, yet he always felt at ease with her. Perhaps he told himself it was the fear, or the knowledge that no matter how many times he saw her he would always end up having to say goodbye.

They sat down in a corner out of the way of the few prying eyes the Yentob had. Joe placed her hand in his as they sipped their drinks. He was glad to see her, more than glad overwhelmed.

So they talked. She asked him if he was still scared of her, telling him as she always did that she was just little old Loren. She told him a lot during their time at the Yentob, really opening up to him for what must have been the first time. She would always feel guilt meeting him even though she knew her relationship with Adrian was over. It was just something she couldn't shake in her head. She was married so it made her feel like she was doing something wrong. Joe guessed in a way she was, they both were, but the situation wasn't exactly simple. It wasn't like she would ever kick Adrian out. She wasn't strong enough and despite everything he did she still cared deeply for her husband and believed he was a fantastic father to their four children. As the conversation moved on they kissed. Loren laughed to Joe telling him she knew he wanted her. Joe simply agreed saying if he had his way he'd clear the table there and then and take her regardless of any audience. He firmly believed that if she called his bluff he would have.

Loren told him about how bad Adrian's gambling was. They had a joint account her money had only just been paid in and Adrian had taken it all out and spent it on a bet. He lost. Normally she told Joe she would be up in arms, but this time she had just ignored it, Adrian had yet to tell her the money was gone. She had checked though she knew full well what had happened.

Then she started to tell him about her mother, her name was Maureen. Loren said that she had been the closest to her out of the three daughters. Just before the end when the cancer took her she became really reclusive. Loren would visit her every week, they'd talk about everything, her mother really opening to her daughter, but whenever someone else would come into the room she would go quiet. Why don't you ever talk to me when anyone else is around Loren would ask her mother? The only reply she ever got was a sigh. Then the cancer took hold of her she wasn't even strong enough to speak then one night she never woke up. She went peacefully, but it shattered Loren completely. That's why she found it hard to open up to anyone, even Joe who she cared about deeply. She was falling for him and it scared her like nothing else she had ever felt. Then there was the guilt she felt because she was still married. It confused her completely she told Joe over and over again as he held her close kissing her lightly. He felt so sad, felt like crying. He wished there were some words he could say to make things okay. There were no words though.

"I remember after the funeral. We had the wake at the house," Loren began telling Joe. "Adrian didn't seem to care. He seemed more interested in a golf game that was on the telly as he had put a big bet on the day of my mother's funeral. I was furious. It was the one time he should have been there for me, and all he could do was stare at the box complaining about the noise we were all making. My entire family was there. I ended up marching up the stairs. Having a blazing row with Adrian before eventually I broke down. I locked myself in the bathroom upstairs refusing to come out. I had taken a bottle of wine with me. I drank it and passed out."

"I don't know what to say. I just want to be there for you," Joe told her squeezing her gently.

"It's ok." She told him wiping tears from her eyes. "Anyway it's made me stronger. I used to be a good little house wife and do as I was told now he knows not to mess with me, especially when I have had a drink. So enough of this talk of doom and gloom kiss me Joe, either that or take me now, but you better do something to cheer me up."

Joe kissed her fiercely. They were both very emotional. He was glad that she felt so at ease that she could open up to him. He knew it must have been hard for her to let go. They sat there for ten minutes before Loren moved away from him sliding her bag over her shoulder.

"Come on let's go outside, get some fresh air before I have to get back to the shop."

Holding hands as they always did they left out the back entrance of the Yentob where they began to kiss passionately. It was a hot, but windy day so Loren used her long brown suede jacket to shield them as they kissed. Joe couldn't help get turned on after the emotional chat they had shared, he found himself touching her breast, before he knew it she had lifted up her top in broad daylight and he was sucking at her nipples. Then his hands moved down instinctively going into her jeans.

"What are you doing in my pussy?" she howled in delight. "Get your hands out." That was not what's she wanted Joe knew that without question as her hands went into his own jeans and she moved her hips with rhythm.

The kissed even more passionately then. Their tongues going back and forth as the heat between them seemed to ignite their bodies. Loren pushed Joe away, tucking her breasts back inside her bra as she tidied herself up. "Joe I do believe you want me." She smiled.

"I always want you every time I see you," he smiled back grabbing her by the neck kissing her again.

She took him by the hand leading him across the road into an alley. He had no idea where they were going. He had never been to Wylde Green before in his life. The alley turned out to be a complete dead end. Leaning against the railings of a fence that ran along one side of the secluded alley they began kissing again. They were touching each other again in the most intimate ways.

"You want to fuck me, don't you Joe?" she asked him as she moaned at the pleasure of having his fingers inside her.

"You know I do. But when we spend our first night together I want it to be right and so do you, not down some back alley." Joe had gotten used to the dirty talk Loren always tried to shock him with. She would always say things she knew could drive him wild knowing full well she was always in full control wherever they were.

"I'm going to have to go in a minute," she sighed. "Adrian will be coming to pick me up from the shop in about an hour."

"It's ok," Joe told her as they tidied themselves up. "I wasn't expecting things to go so far but well at least I know you fancy me regardless of drink. We are both pretty sober. I just expected to talk maybe kiss," he laughed.

"Adrian is taking the kids out to watch the football tonight. So we can talk for most of the night."

"That's great," he told her as she led him out the alley.

"Well you had better go that way to your bus stop, "she laughed. "And I had better shake my ass back to the shop.

"How you going to explain how late you were? You have been gone over two and a half hours."

"Don't worry I will sort it," she smiled, and at that their time together was over, at least until the evening when she would be home alone.

Around seven o'clock they both logged onto chat. Loren called Joe first to let him know Adrian had taken the kids out to the football match. They turned the web camera's on as normal, but it just wasn't the same. Joe said it was like being in a silent movie not being able to talk to her so he decided after about 15 minutes of trying to chat; but just the two of them staring at each other, to call her up.

"It's funny," he told her," but it feels weird talking on chat when I can just phone you."

"You really turned me on today Joe," she said smiling at him through the camera. I'm going to have to go play with my rabbit later while thinking of you."

Joe laughed at that. Loren had often talked of how she used her vibrator when she got a quiet moment. It was easier for him to believe she didn't sleep with her husband the way she talked about how marvellous her electrical rabbit was between her legs.

"Wouldn't you prefer the real thing?" Joe asked her unable to stop himself smirking.

"You know I would," she sighed. After they had chatted for another ten minutes about how things were good between them again Loren did what she always did, she shocked Joe. "Look I'm going to have to go play with my rabbit," she smiled. "Call me in ten minutes if you want to listen in." At that Loren logged off leaving Joe sitting gob smacked on his stool. He decided without hesitation that he would gladly listen in, and he wouldn't wait ten minutes either. Rushing to the caravan Joe lay down on the bed. He called Loren up.

"Hello," she sighed.

"What you doing?" he asked unbuttoning his jeans as he held himself. He was stiff and dripping with wanting for her.

"What do you think?" Loren replied the sound of her voice unable to hide the noise of the battery powered rabbit as it went to work inside her.

Joe simply listened as he masturbated. He told Loren what he was doing as she described the sensation of the rabbit. She told him in detail how it worked how she used it to pleasure herself. Joe was amazingly turned on by it. He couldn't believe what they were doing. He could hear her moaning and sighing as she placed the vibrating rabbits head inside her going deeper. Joe imagined as he touched himself that it was he and not the rabbit inside Loren. It was him making her moan with every movement of his hips, thrusting deep inside her. She told him how it had special ears, her little rabbit, that teased her most sensitive areas. Then as her moans grew louder she bid Joe goodnight saying she had to finish herself off. After that Adrian would be home with the kids. She only wished it was Joe she had and not her battery operated toy. As she hung up Joe lost all interest in what he was doing. He didn't want to touch himself he wanted to be making love to the woman he had fallen for so deeply.

After that day at the Yentob their relationship grew. They spoke online as often as they could. Checkers was still their excuse, but it was a good excuse that met their needs. Loren's comments online would always border on the tantalisingly cheeky whenever Adrian was not around. If her husband popped out the room or wasn't looking at what she was doing she would turn an innocent comment of Joe's into something sexual knowing full well Joe wouldn't be able to response by typing anything less than innocent back himself in case they got caught. Whatever arguments they had shared in the past Joe could no longer remember them. Things between them had become strong. Loren had finally after all the long waiting opened up to him. Joe believed despite the fact she had yet to say the words that she really did love him. When she called him up From Hope Springs they chatted for hours about anything that crossed their minds. They wanted to see each other again. They just didn't know when. Joe didn't want to broach the subject for fear of Loren backing off yet again. Then one day Loren eventually told Adrian she was off out for another night with the girls despite his protests. It was not a night with the girls she had planned though, or a night out with Joe for that matter. This time they had planned to spend an intimate evening together. Joe would cook for her. Then he would take her in his arms, to his bed where he would make love to her for the first time.

The day had arrived. Joe had invited Loren down to the caravan for an intimate evening. They both agreed it was what they wanted. Joe's parents weren't too thrilled about the whole thing. He hadn't been able to keep the fact he was seeing a married woman from them. They were in and out of the kitchen all the time. They had seen him constantly chatting to Loren. His mother, Rosetta, seemed more understanding than his father who simply said that it just wasn't something you did. The woman was married, more than likely would always be married and you just didn't do that; was his father's stance on things. Joe knew his father was right. Still the world was never easy. Life was never simple and he loved Loren completely.

The evening before he had made sure he had everything ready for their meal, just a simple thing, meatballs and pasta covered in melted cheese. The meatballs proved almost impossible to find, even though they were just the plain old tinned variety. He bought a bottle of vodka for them to share. With it he got some orange Juice for Loren and some coke for himself. He was all prepared he just had to make it through the day.

That day at work he couldn't concentrate. He rarely if ever had kept his private life secret from those he worked with. During his time of internet bed hopping he had been jokingly labelled a slag, not to mention a gypsy due to his life in the caravan, as well as many other nicknames he just laughed off. Everyone knew Loren would be going back to Joe's for a meal. He planned to cook her something simple. They would eat despite his father's protests to the contrary in the kitchen of his parent's house. He had a terrible cold coming on. All day he fought is as best he could with everything from hot lemon drinks to cough sweets. Anything he could think of he tried. The night before he had taken several pain killers, wrapped up in 2 jumpers and gone to sleep covered in Vapour rub.

By lunchtime he wasn't feeling any better, but luckily he wasn't feeling much worse either and was just hoping he could make it through the night. It was obvious they would make love it was what they both wanted. Joe just wanted to try and make the night as special for Loren as he could. Around three thirty he started getting texts from Loren on the mobile phone she carried with her outside of work, the one she used at home. She was missing him the texts told him. Joe did his best to reply even though for him he wasn't even supposed to have his mobile switched on let alone be texting anyone. He texted her back telling him he hoped to see her soon. Through her texts he found she had left the charity shop in Wylde Green and gone for a quick drink with a friend. Then she had made her way into town and was now drinking in the pub they had met at for lunch a few times before. The idea of eating a meal in his parent's house was evaporating fast. He had grown to know Loren very well over the last few months. He knew her well enough to know that she would have put quite a few drinks away by the time five o'clock rolled around. It was bad enough that his father disapproved. He had no intention of letting them meet Loren while she was intoxicated with more than a few vodkas in her system. Of course he always got the shakes when he saw his soul mate. Also the fact he was fighting off a heavy cold would push back any ideas of food he may have had.

Five o'clock had never taken so long to arrive, and when it did Joe had never been happier. Loren had been constantly texting him. The last text was to tell him she was cold and waiting at the top of the hill from where his office was.

He walked up the road with his work mate Larry. Larry had been a great friend and always there on the end of the phone to support Joe when he needed to talk about his troubles with Loren. Now Larry would meet her if only briefly. When they got to the top of the hill that broke into Colmore Row Loren was there waiting. She took Joe's hand instantly smiling that ever so infectious smile that made him happy to be alive. Larry and Loren exchanged brief hello's before Joe got them into a taxi so that they could get straight back to his caravan.

"How are you, Joe?" she asked him her face wearing a broad grin that said she was in full control of the situation.

"I'll be fine when I stop shaking," he laughed. She always made him shake and he couldn't get over why. He had never been nervous of all the other women he had been with.

"I don't know why you're always so scared of me. I'm just me." She told him briefly kissing him on the lips.

They spent the taxi ride home talking about pretty much nothing. Just idling away the time. Joe did the usual thing of asking her how things were with the kids, how things were at home. Loren gave him the usual response of telling him everything was fine and that once again she had told Adrian she was having a night out with the girls. While Adrian didn't like it, and Joe knew this from the arguments he knew were going on as he chatted to her the night before online, Loren was getting stronger when it came to dealing with her husband.

It wasn't long before they reached Kings Norton, the caravan, and the eventual night of intimacy that awaited them. Joe paid for the taxi as they got out and ushered his love into the caravan.

He turned on the lights as Loren sat down upon the bed taking off her shoes. Pouring them both a glass of wine he told her they could eat whenever she was ready. The only hunger that was in either of their eyes was for each other and no food would be eaten that night.

Handing her a glass of wine he put on some music he knew she would like. He had a few CD's that contained a mix of sixties and seventies tunes which were Loren's favourites. Within no time at all Loren starting to relax and they were dancing like two mad people in the caravan the music blaring to the disapproval of Joe's parents. Still they knew he was home and never once came knocking that night.

At one point when it had grown slightly dark Joe even led Loren outside where the music could still be heard. It was raining lightly and they danced outside like the carefree souls that they were.

"You're mad," laughed Loren as she held hands, dancing with him in the rain. "You're just like me."

Joe just smiled leading her back to the caravan and another glass of wine. She sat back on the bed with Joe facing her. God she was beautiful. She slowly removed her top smiling at him all the while, she motioned for Joe to come towards her as they began to kiss and Joe fiddled with the straps of her bra seeking out her breasts with his lips. Then she was up again playing more songs, teasing Joe as she paraded around the caravan topless. He let her play her music, and watched her dance for him. Then when he could take no more he pulled her to the bed unbuttoning her jeans as he removed his own clothes. They kissed slowly at first, and then as their passion grew so did their kisses. Joe reached for some protection that he had put at the corner of the bed.

"What do you think you're doing?"

"Sorry," Joe replied. "I just thought it's what we both want."

"It's ok I'm just messing. I do want you. Just me and Adrian have never used them. I've never... We don't sleep together any more like I say." Besides it's a pretty safe time now I've just come off my period. Besides If you want me to leave Adrian you will have to get me pregnant." She laughed at that smiling as she sat cross legged on the opposite side of the bed. Joe couldn't help but stare at her. Her eyes always sparkled. They were her best feature and she knew it as she had told Joe every man that had ever tried chatting her up always mentioned her lovely eyes. He always felt so helpless with Loren. He had a nagging fear every day that one day he would lose her for good. The amount of times she would treat their relationship like a yo-yo made him worry that one day the proverbial string would snap, with her never to return again.

Hearing her talk of pregnancy Joe should have heard alarm bells ringing all around him. Instead he found himself liking the idea of Loren bearing his child. If he was honest with himself he had thought about it a great deal. He had never wanted to have children with Isobel. Despite the fact that he loved Reece completely his son had been unplanned. Isobel had talked of having another child during the five years that they were together, even bargaining with him telling him he could go out more if he gave her a second child. He had considered it at the time as his life was so empty. He never really had much of a social life during his time with Isobel. As his feelings had quickly grown with Loren he had realized that if he were ever to have another child he would want it to be with her. Dropping the protection from his hands he moved closer to Loren laying down upon her. He played with her then, getting her aroused, hearing her moan in eager delight, before he entered her slowly. He teased her at first with his tip not wanting to rush their first time, wanting to make sure she was ready.

Loren was ready. She let Joe know by moving her hips up to slowly meet his so that he couldn't do anything else but enter her. She smiled with that first moment. They both just stared at each other realizing it had finally happened. They were making love for the first time. It was special for both of them.

He began thrusting himself slowly inside her gazing into her innocent looking face as he did. Their eyes were deadlocked. With each and every thrust of their hips they simply stared at each other.

"I love you Loren Green," he told her.

"And I love you Joe Hughes." Came her breathless reply as she felt him press himself deep inside her.

"Do you really?" he asked wondering if she was just saying the words because he wanted to hear them, because they were making love.

"I would never say anything like that if I didn't mean it Joe. I know I keep my guard up but I've let myself go with you and now I can't seem to stop it. I do love you Joe."

Joe threw the covers aside he wanted to see all the beauty of Loren her whole body. He wanted to be able to kiss every single inch of her.

"Don't do that Joe" she told him quietly, all the while moaning with pleasure. "I don't like my body. Ever since Harriet was born I've had terrible stretch marks."

"It's natural."

"You can't like what you see I look horrible," she sighed as Joe sat up circling his fingers lightly around the stretch marks upon her tummy.

Her hand instinctively went to Joe to stop him. "Adrian wouldn't even touch me after Harriet was born. I know we had more kids after but my body disgusted him. He was more interested in me just pleasuring him. I hate my body."

"I love it. Look you look fantastic to me. You have the best body I have ever seen. I mean put it this way just imagine your stomach is a beach. If you run your hand through it you get ripples, but it doesn't diminish the beauty of what is there."

Joe kissed her breasts, slowly moving down to remove her hand which she had placed over her stomach, kissing her slowly. Eventually he moved down further his tongue moving between her legs. This was something new to Joe, he had rarely gone down on any woman, not even Isobel. It was something he hated doing. With Loren it was something he wanted to do. Once he had started he couldn't stop. He didn't just lick but suck. He explained his own insecurities to Loren, mentioning once more about his tongue tied years as a child as he asked her for instruction. She came a few minutes later as Joe brought her into a climatic frenzy.

"Come here and make love to me Joe she said. She pulled him up towards her as she used the covers of the bed to hide their bodies particularly her own. By then it was only nine thirty, they made love for hours that night with Loren continually telling Joe to fuck her to get her pregnant. Their lovemaking was fun and spontaneous. Whenever Loren would get up to dance or to change the song Joe would be inside her. He took her on the floor, against the caravan cupboard walls. They just couldn't get enough of each other. Adrian eventually text her at around two thirty the following morning. She didn't answer at first. She didn't want to go home. She had no intention of leaving Joe, not after such a magical first time together. After a while with Joe telling, almost begging her not to leave, she text Adrian telling him she was stopping at a female friends for that night but that their marriage was over and she wouldn't be coming back. Her husband sent several more texts but they ignored the beeps of her phone as they continued to make love until they fell asleep in each other's arms both blissfully happy for what would be the first time in their lives.

Joe was supposed to be in work that following morning. He couldn't leave Loren. She had made the biggest decision in her life. She had left Adrian her husband of nearly 18 years. Hesitantly he called work from his mobile, warning Loren to keep quiet. The phone rang out with someone picking up after only two rings. Joe wasn't surprised; it was eight thirty, the phone located on his team leader's desk in front of her very nose.

"Icon Finances, Sally speaking," came the voice of his team leader.

"Hiya. Its Joe," he greeted.

"Morning Joe."

"I can't come in this morning. I haven't been able to shake that cold and also I have been throwing up all morning."

"Well how did it go last night? I bet your lady friend wasn't too impressed."

"She was very understanding. She left early saying we could always do it another night," Joe lied as he playfully ran his fingers through Loren's hair as she lay quietly beside him.

"Ok Joe, hope you get better soon," Sally said over the phone," Give us a call tomorrow if you still don't feel any better."

At that Sally hung up. Joe looked over at Loren, smiling. She returned his smile with a look of sorrow shining in her eyes.

"I miss my kids," she moaned. "I don't know what I'm going to do."

"It will be ok," he told her wondering if it really would. "You have done the hardest part."

By the time they got dressed it was around nine. Loren had simply laid in bed for an hour a look of complete sadness on her face. She was torn between staying with Joe, or going back to see her kids. It was obvious she would have to face Adrian sooner, rather than later. They took a walk around Kings Norton. Joe had told her that the best thing they could do after their long night of drinking was to get some fresh air. So they left the caravan behind. Loren kept asking him what she could do. He didn't have any answers. He hadn't expected her to leave Adrian so suddenly. He was over the moon that she had but he had nowhere that she could realistically stay, though he did tell her she could stop with him at the caravan that night if she needed to regardless of what his parents might think, or say. She eventually decided she would try and call her father, (her step dad) who was supposed to be working. He was a driver for a supermarket in Kings Heath. She would stay at his for a few nights until she got herself sorted. Her father would drive her up to the house so she could collect some clothes, see her kids, and sort things with her husband.

When she called the store she was told her father wasn't there. He was out making deliveries so Loren did the only other thing she could think of which was to call her husband to talk things over.

"It's over, Joe heard her tell Adrian. Joe could only hear one side of the conversation. The longer it went on the worse it seemed to get. Adrian was convincing her to come home.

"Look I stopped over at a friends I'm fine. No we are finished I always give you second chances. If I come back we live separate lives completely. I will come back for the kids until I can get a place of my own." At that Loren hung up. Joe didn't know what to say all he could do is go to her and hold her.

"Do you think I made the right decision?" she asked him.

"It's not for me to say. I think you made a big decision last night. I know you miss your kids but you know if you go back you won't ever leave."

"No things will be different."

"Last night you said you loved me. Do you?" he asked.

"Yes"
"So say it."

"I love you Joe. You know I do."

"So what now will we still be able to talk?"

"Not for a while no. At least not online."

So they walked back to Joe's. Loren waited in the caravan as Joe fixed them both a cup of tea. Loren smiled telling him it was a rare thing for anyone to ever make her a cup of tea. Such a simple thing thought Joe.

He called her a taxi, as he sat there holding her hand. She was supposed to be in work for one o'clock that day, but called in sick on her mobile. Then the Taxi arrived. Joe followed her out of the caravan wishing her good luck. She promised she would stick to her story no matter how much pressure her husband put her under.

"Besides," she told Joe, "When I get in I'm going straight to bed I'm shattered."

Joe was tired himself so when Loren left he went straight to bed. He slept through most of what remained of the day. At just after three he was woken by the ringing of his mobile. It was Loren.

"Hello," Joe said. He felt groggy having just woken up from his long sleep. "Are you okay?"

"I had to tell Adrian," she blurted out her words.

"What do you mean? I thought we had agreed. You told him you had stayed at a friends! This is only going to make things worse." Joe wasn't worried about himself. He had no fear of Loren's husband. He would have welcomed the chance to meet him face to face, tell him exactly what he thought of him. Joe didn't understand what had happened when she had gone back home, but he knew he was about to find out.

"He kept pressuring me. Asking who exactly it was I stayed with. He wanted a number. So in the end I had no choice. I had to tell him. I told him how many times we made love that it wasn't a one off thing that we care about each other. He knows it's over between me, and him but you can understand I will need some time things will be difficult for us at the moment."

"Did he hit you though? Are you okay?"

"No. He didn't. I did tell him I was scared that he might as I went back. He has been very calm, and understanding. I just wanted you to know I was ok." At that she hung up leaving Joe's head spinning with questions. Where on earth did they go from there?

Joe didn't go back to work for the rest of that week, or the week after. He rarely heard from Loren and spent most of his time sleeping or texting her. She eventually called him telling him he needed to calm down. What was she supposed to do? she asked him. Should she just tell her husband she was off to see her lover? It wasn't as simple as that. Joe needed to respect her space. She was angry he had been texting her constantly. The thing was it wasn't her that would read the texts but her husband. She was suffering severe migraines, having spent the last few days in bed and had no way of knowing Joe had been trying to contact her. They grew distant after that. It was happening all over again. Joe returned to work the following week with Loren calling him up every three or four days telling him that she was missing him but that Adrian knew she was calling. Then one evening he came home from work to check his emails to find a message from Adrian waiting for him on Chatsmart

"Why don't you just leave us alone? I don't know what Loren has told you but we are fine. Our marriage isn't perfect but whose is? She isn't the person you seem to think she is. When she is online she has cybersex on online with other men, and the day after she slept with you we had sex. I'm not angry with you, in a way I pity you. She is just using you. You would be better off leaving her alone."

Reading the message Joe was furious. He refused to believe Loren would have slept with her husband. Would she really do that to him? Then reality dawned on him. He had slept with women while still married to Isobel but he and his wife still had sex. How foolish was he to believe that Loren didn't have sex with her husband. He decided to send Adrian a message back.

I don't believe a word of your lies. If it's true get Loren to call me.

Five minutes later his phone rang with Loren on the other end.

"So you two are playing silly buggers messaging each other are you?" she asked.

"Me? No your husband fucking well is," Joe told her. He read out the email Adrian had sent him. "So is any of that true?"

"Yes I did sleep with him. He said after sleeping with you I owed him a shag. So I thought it's only sex why not." Loren told him angrily.

"You owed him one?" Joe screamed down the phone in disbelief."

"Well now you both hate me," sighed Loren, "He is laughing now." She was right of course. Joe could hear Adrian putting in his two cents worth, laughing at the argument he was causing.

"Well tell him from me that I haven't changed my mind about you. Whatever he hoped to achieve by sending me that email has failed. I will not give up on you."

"Did you hear that Adrian," she said talking to her husband. "Joe said you haven't put him off with your little games."

"So what about the cybersex?" laughed Joe?

"That's bullshit. He is just stirring." Loren told him.

"So you hate me now?" Adrian said from the other side of Loren's phone.

"I don't feel anything for you Adrian. I told you before if we didn't have the kids I would have left you ages ago. If it wasn't for the kids I would be with Joe not you. And also while Joe is on the phone what did I say to you after we had sex?"

"You said it would never happen again," Joe heard Adrian sighing in the background. "I've lost everything," he added.

"It's not a game," Joe replied.

"Ooh he seems to think it is. Messaging you causing trouble. There are enough arguments here without him causing more."

"Ok well just as long as we are okay. I mean it has upset me, but well I've been married myself."

"I'll call you tomorrow in the morning ok Joe?"

"OK night Loren."

She didn't call that next day as she said she would. Joe left her a message online hoping to get a response. He could have called her mobile, but feared doing so would only aggravate her situation with Adrian. So Joe waited. He kept himself busy with selling things online. He knew he would eventually have to return to work. He only hoped that things between him and Loren would resolve quickly. It was two days later that she did call. Adrian knew what she was doing. Whether he liked it or not was another thing entirely. She missed Joe a great deal. Admitted communication was hard now that her husband knew all about them. She wouldn't be able to see Joe again until after she had moved out. Once she got her own place they could see each other properly, go on dates with no more sneaking around. Joe didn't like what he was hearing one bit. He missed Loren as though she were a part of him that was missing. He pressed her again on why she had slept with Adrian. It was burning him up inside. It wasn't just about jealously. They had made love for the first time only days before then she went off and slept with her husband. Joe wanted to understand it but couldn't. Loren did her best to explain even though she spent most of the time doing that shouting at him. She told him it had just been sex and that she was basically forced into it. There had been no intimacy and Adrian hadn't come inside her. She told Joe this saying she hoped he would understand how it had been for her. Joe still didn't understand, if she was forced into it then surely she would have reported him. Still Joe knew how abuse worked with married couples. He had never had any physical abuse from Isobel, but mental abuse yes, he believed over the years he had suffered much of that. He knew from past experience that there was no arguing with her. If anything serious was ever to happen between them it would be in Loren's own time. Joe just hoped that would be soon. He did argue with her about it, but soon realised that as per normal he was wasting his breath. She told him in no uncertain terms she would be doing what was right for her and not let any tell her what to do ever again. Joe reminded her how he had never told her what to do. Joe loved her for the person she was. Joe always expected nothing less than that she always be herself when with him. So the conversation ended with Joe agreeing as he had done so many times before to give her space. They would still be able to chat when she was at work, but their online time was now officially finished. Adrian would not stand for her sitting chatting to Joe for hours as she had done for the past four months.

When they both returned to work they were able to talk on the phone again. It was a strain for both of them. Loren insisted if she could find a way to see Joe she would. It was impossible for the time being, Joe knew that. So he kept himself busy like he always did. He had Reece at the weekends, even having overnight an extra week or two while things didn't seem to be getting better with Loren. He spoke to Amanda more hoping she could give him some good advice. One evening Amanda told him how her friend had been dropping out of the Salsa classes she had been going to. Joe offered to go with her. So Joe had a social life again. He arranged to go to the cinema with his work friends and he would try Salsa with Amanda. If nothing else it would be a fun evening. He told Loren all about his Salsa night he had arranged with Amanda. Loren was absolutely fine with it telling Joe to have a good night.

    The night Joe had arranged to go to a salsa class with his friend Amanda who lived in Rubery arrived. He took a bus straight from work to her house. Joe had always wanted to learn to dance; besides he told himself it would take his mind off Loren for a few hours which had to be a good thing. He had told Loren he was going, and she knew he was just a friend to Amanda, nothing more.

    When he got to Amanda's she cooked him dinner. As usual it was a feast that Joe felt obliged to finish. There was steak with potatoes, tons of vegetables, covered in lashings of gravy. Joe wondered if he would be able to dance to any ability on such a full stomach.

The dance classes were held at a small dance studio just a short drive from Amanda's. The place looked like what Joe guessed a dance studio must look like having never been to one in his life. The building had yellow walls with a triangular roof. Inside there was just a small corridor with the entrance to the studio's toilet facilities before it opened up behind a screen wall to the dance floor which was roughly ten meters by fifteen meters long. Large mirrors ran along each side of the dance floor while in one corner stood a large barrel of drinking water.

When they arrived the previous class was just finishing. This Amanda explained to him was the intermediate class. They would be doing the beginners. Joe just looked on amazed it all looked very complicated to him. As far as he was concerned he had two left feet. He had only come out with Amanda as the friend she usually went to Salsa with had let her down on the last two occasions leaving her to dance alone.

They waited about ten minutes for the intermediate class to end with more people showing up for the beginner's class. Amanda pointed out that she recognised a few of them as fellow council workers. There were only about seven couples in total including them, but Joe hadn't expected there to be many people. After all they were hardly in the city centre. If the studio had been up town it would most likely have been packed. Still with less people it made it easier for the instructor to teach his pupils how to salsa.

The instructor was a young fair haired guy dressed very smartly in white shirt, and black trousers. He looked a good few years younger than Joe, but Joe thought he looked every bit the professional he had expected.

Amanda whispered to him from his side that usually the instructor, who introduced himself as Ian, had his partner with him. Apparently she was a very gorgeous wafer thin girl that together with her other half danced amazingly well. Good enough for TV Amanda added to Joe.

With the music starting to play the young instructor got everyone to go over the basics. Joe hadn't a clue what he was doing at first, but soon picked things up. As the night went on he was amused to find Amanda doing things backwards. She was following what the instructor was teaching them by looking into the mirrors which meant she got everything in reverse. Eventually the both got the hang of things. Joe found himself having a great night. Every so often they would swap partners, so Joe found that he danced with all the ladies in attendance that night. Along with singing, which Joe only managed at Karaoke level, dancing was something he had always wanted to learn. Joe found that he really enjoyed the evening. When it eventually ended with the instructor thanking everyone for coming Joe found himself feeling a bit sad. He wanted more. He hoped Amanda would let him come with her again.

Amanda drove him home after Salsa. They talked about Loren for the first time that night. All his friend could say on the subject was that the woman seemed very confused. Amanda had once been in a similar situation. She told Joe that at the end of the day Loren could only leave for her, not him. It would be the hardest decision of the woman's life and she didn't believe for one minute that it would happen anytime soon. As far as she was concerned Joe had a very long wait ahead of him if that's what he really wanted to do, otherwise he was better off finding himself someone less complicated to share his life with.

Back at home Joe sat at his stool on his PC. The place was like a second home for him. He had lost count of the amount of times one of his parents had told him to take a break from all his ebaying.

"You should go out with your friends more. Get a social life," they would often say to him.

Of course it wasn't that simple. Whenever he did go out it was usually just to the cinema with a few friends from work. Loren would end up calling up if she was at work. No matter what he was doing or when she was always on his mind. It made concentration the hardest thing for Joe to come by. Salsa with Amanda had been a refreshing change. So as he logged onto Chatsmart he was not at all surprised to see he had three messages from Loren.

I'm bored. I bet you're out having a great time, the first message read. I'm really pissed off; the second message said speaking for itself. The third message was a simple apology for the first two messages. Logging onto chat Joe found Loren there waiting.

"Had a good night?" she typed. She invited him to share the cameras straight away.

"Yes I did thanks. You knew I was at Salsa with Amanda. What's with all the messages? I went out had a great night. Did nothing wrong, and now I feel guilty for that?" Joe typed back as he accepted her camera invitation. He could tell by the look on her face she had been drinking. Loren always tended to miss him more when she had drunk a few glasses of wine.

"Tell me how to make money on Ebay Joe. What really sells?"

"Why on earth do you what to know that?" typed Joe puzzled. "Has Adrian put you up to this? It's not as easy as just knowing what to sell it takes hard work. I have been doing it for over twelve months.

"Adrian isn't here he has gone out." Loren typed. Joe knew straight away she was lying. He could tell from the sideways look she was giving to her off screen husband that he was there. Her face always turned into a snarl when she spoke to Adrian.

"I know he is there. What is this all about?"

At that chaos broke out as Joe watched in horror as Loren's laptop disappeared from view. Adrian was obviously there. Joe had no doubt as he watched an unseen second person throw the laptop to the floor. He waited five minutes before Loren came back online.

"What the hell is going on?"

"We are having an argument. He doesn't want me speaking to you."

"Well then let's just leave it for now. Don't let him provoke you."

At that the camera went off again as more fighting broke out between the married couple. Joe wished he knew where they lived. If he had the address he would most certainly have called the police at that time. He feared for Loren's safety, he knew full well from his first meeting with Loren what Adrian was capable of. Her husband had hit her several times before. Joe was scared that this time it might lead to something fatal.

Five minutes later his phone rang. A number showed up on the digital display. It was Loren on her home phone. She had forgotten to withhold the number.

"Are you okay?" Joe asked getting very worried.

"I'm fine he's just throwing his weight around. I packed my bag earlier tonight. I was going to leave, but he talked me out of it as usual. What would you have done if I had turned up at your door?"

"I would have invited you in, and made you a cup of tea," laughed Joe. "You know that I would never let you down."

"It's good to know I have someone like that there for me. Thank you Joe."

"So how are things now?"

"Not good. I think he has accepted things are over. He is very upset. Look can I still come with you to the concert?" Loren asked him.

"Well I do have a mate going with me now to be honest," Joe told her, "But I can make an excuse." Joe had asked his friend Alex to go with him. He didn't know what he would tell her but Alex knew the ticket had always been intended for Loren and would understand. "If you want to still go to the concert you can."

"Yes I really would like to go, and I know how much it means to you, Joe."

"Yes we have been waiting a long time for this night."

"Well you don't need to worry anymore. I have told Adrian I am going with you. If he doesn't like it I have told him I will walk right now."

"So now what?"

"I have to go. I'm going to have to have a big talk with Adrian sort things out once and for all but I will text you in the morning to let you know how things are. Harriet walked in just now she knows I'm seeing someone else. Adrian told her. He didn't say who, but my daughter's not stupid Joe."

"I don't want the kids to hate me."

"They won't. They have always liked you Joe."

"Ok well you know I love you and I think you love me too don't you?"

"Yes I think so?"

"And your marriage is definitely over now and that's what you want?"

"Yes it is. Good night Joe. You get some sleep."

"Night Loren," Joe hung up. He was knackered. He looked at the clock on his PC. It was nearly 2 in the morning. Had they really been talking that long? He really did need to get some rest. He would have a long day ahead of him, as well as a very long night knowing Loren. He didn't feel one hundred percent either. Joe felt as though he had a cold coming on. He went to the caravan smothered himself in vapour rub and fell asleep. He felt calm for the first time in a long while.

That previous night had left Joe completely drained. With everything that had gone on after he got back from Salsa with Amanda he was pretty much wiped out. Still it had all been worth it. Loren had finally told Adrian where to go. Insisting to her husband that she would never get back with him and despite that fact that she was living with him, she would indeed be going to see Darren Hayes with Joe that following evening. So despite her husband's tantrums everything had worked out for the best. Harriet had seemingly found out that her mother was seeing another man after walking in on her mother and father arguing. The eldest of Loren's children didn't seem to have taken it badly from what Loren had told him in the early hours of the morning. Joe hadn't had any sleep save a few hours. He doubted he would get much that night what with the concert. But he would sleep the following day. It was all worth a few sleepless nights having things work out for the better at last.

They met at the top of Colmore Row as they had done before. As always she grabbed Joe's hand, smiling. It was as if she was saying you're all mine Joe Hughes. They walked to the train station talking about that previous night. Joe told her how scared he had been for her.

"It was lucky I don't know where you live," he confessed. "If I had your address I would have sent the police around when Adrian threw the laptop across the kitchen."

"Well that wouldn't have been good for the kids," she said smiling squeezing his hand gently. They kissed against a pillar on the train platform until the train arrived before finding themselves a seat. They were on their way.

"I heard Darren Hayes playing the other day just after I had taken the kids to school," Loren told him as they sat on the train.

"And you missed me didn't you. Bet it made you feel really sad," Joe said with a cocky tone to his voice. "Admit it."

"Fuck off," came her reply, she couldn't help but laugh. She knew Joe was right. Loren had been trying to keep away from Joe, but the more she did the more she missed him. There were so many songs they had shared, so many moments it was hard not to think about the man that had come into her life; promising to give her the romance only seen in the movies. "Okay maybe just a little bit," she conceded kissing him lightly.

When the train pulled up into Wolverhampton train station they got out walking along the platform until they came to the exit.

"I can't believe we finally made it," Joe told her as they walked up the road towards Wolverhampton town centre.

"You know I wouldn't have missed this for the world. Besides whom would you have taken if not for me?"

"One of my female friends," Joe replied in dead seriousness.

"Well I'm here now. So let's go find somewhere to have a drink."

"Good idea," Joe told her. "The civic hall doesn't open till seven, and the concert won't start till eight at least. Then you have the support first so I'd say we have a good few hours pub time ahead of us."

They walked on towards the civic noticing a queue that trailed back from the entrance to over a dozen shops. There was no way they would be going into the civic until everyone else had gone in. They had pre booked seats so didn't need to worry. They went to one of the local bars called the Hen and Parrot.

Joe found them somewhere to sit and ordered them a pint of lager each. They talked about how things would get better. Loren admitted to being jealous of Amanda.

"Don't worry. Whenever you go out I'll make sure I do too," she smiled.

"It's not like when you get yourself sorted you will be able to go out all the time," commented Joe. "It's going to be very hard."

"I know that, but I will do it."

"I'm just glad after last night things have worked out between me and you. You know when we are together we are unstoppable."

"Well I'm here aren't I?"

"That you are." Joe kissed her as he got up. He went to the bar deciding to order them something special. He noticed a shooters menu. They were one pound each so he bought six, two of each flavour. They knocked them back straight away.

Loren grimaced at one. She hated the flavour. She pulled a face in disgust.

"That was terrible," she said.

"Yeah but it will get us pissed quicker laughed Joe, "Besides we won't drink much when we are in the civic so might as well make the most of things for now."

They eventually left the Hen and Parrot after one more Lager. Their next stop was the local Yates bar. Loren spotted a pool table so they decided to play pool. Joe had never been any good at pool. Luckily Loren was just as bad as him. They weren't playing for any other reason than fun. Joe loved the fact that they were out enjoying themselves. Loren was the only woman he had ever met who he was sexually attracted to that he enjoyed spending time with that didn't involve sex. He had female friends that he spent time with, but Loren was always more than that, and he cherished every moment he had with her. Just to do something simple like holding her hand made him smile. He watched Loren take her shots on the pool table, feeling so proud to be out with her. The idea of whether or not they would go to the concert together had been always been hit and miss. He never believed they would actually make it. He felt it was some kind of miracle that they had got that far. It was a good sign after all the arguing the night before. He had been so worried that Adrian would have done her serious harm that night.

After playing pool they sat down in the corner of Yates's drinking double vodka's. As usual Loren asked him what he saw in her. She always seemed to be fishing in that way. It was like she could never understand that he did love her. She had never been able to say she loved him since that first time, even though the previous night he had asked her if she did, and she had agreed. Loren had never said the words though. All she would say was that she really cared about him. Joe could only look at her feeling really sad. Surely after all that time she must have known how she felt about him. He decided to drop the subject telling her it was time they made their way to the civic.

As they walked out Loren told him how this was his night. She knew how important the concert was to him.

"No. It was never about the concert," Joe told her bluntly, "I couldn't care less about that. It's always been about being able to spend time with you.

At that Loren just smiled as they walked hand in hand through the civic doors, both trying to do their very best impression of a sober person. They obviously succeeded as they both got in.

By the time they got seated they had missed the support act. They sat down both smiling happily. Loren had rarely ever been to a concert. Joe was glad that it was something he could do for her.

When Darren Hayes came onto the stage he was shrouded in darkness. The crowd went wild. Everyone stood up. The concert proved every bit as good as the one Joe had taken his sister to nearly a year before. Darren Hayes played all of his best songs from his first album such as insatiable, I Miss you, and Good enough as well as many tracks from his new album, not to mention some of his old songs from when he was in the band Savage Garden. Joe had sent a lot of the songs to Loren when they were on chat together so she had no trouble singing along to Joe with the words. It was the most emotional night of Joe's life. He couldn't look at Loren at one point. Tears of Joy streamed down his face. He had never been so happy.

Wiping the tears away he turned to Loren, kissing her passionately. He was just overwhelmed by the entire night. The build up for the concert had been months. Ever since he had first starting chatting to her with the idea of them doing something special together, he had waited for this night to arrive. When he had originally ordered the tickets he had felt foolish. Joe had never really thought Loren would come out with him to see Darren Hayes play. Then as time went on he thought it was a certainty that she would, only for his hopes to be dashed after the night they made love when she returned to her husband. The concert went on for a good ninety minutes with the usual encore. They didn't stay for that, instead they pressed their bodies against one of the corridor walls as they kissed their passion overwhelming them.

    Leaving the civic they headed for the train station only to find a bar that had a karaoke. They still had a good hour before the last train so they went in. They both loved karaoke. The night just seemed to get better with every single moment they spent together. So ordering drinks they sang on the karaoke, Elvis Presley's Suspicious Minds. Then knowing time was short they headed for the train station. By then Joe was overcome with lust. The monitor on the train station said they had ten minutes before the last train would arrive. Joe dragged Loren into the men's room laying her down on the floor. He had to have her there and then. They made love quickly and passionately before rushing as they heard the sound of the train pulling into the station. It was then that Joe noticed a change in Loren. She was feeling bad about the sex. Joe didn't know why. She had been just as keen as him to have him inside her. He wondered if she had told Adrian that that night was supposed to be their last together. Perhaps she had told her husband that she would go out with Joe, but that nothing would happen between them. If that was the case then that deal had been broken now.

The train ride back was an almost silent one. Loren's mood had changed. She received a text that Joe was unable to read. She deleted it almost immediately. Joe presumed it was from Adrian though Loren insisted it had been from her daughter Harriet. Joe moved away, he was angry. He sat on his own for the rest of the ride back into Birmingham. As Loren got off the train she started screaming at Joe. Saying she had had enough, that it was over. Joe couldn't believe what he was hearing. He managed to convince her to come back to his so they could spend some time together.

"It will cost me just as much to get us both a taxi to mine, and then you a Taxi home as it would to get us both separate taxies from town."

So they took a taxi back to Joe's. Through that long ride back Loren moaned that it wasn't right. She kept mentioning how she should be back at home with her kids. That's was the crux of it though. It wasn't about how she felt about Joe. She always felt guilty about not being with her kids. It must have been terrible for her to argue with Adrian the night before only for Harriet, her eldest, to walk in on the explosive scene.

Locking the caravan door behind them Joe did his best to make Loren feel at ease, but she seemed different to him. She sat on the bed then looking towards the window. She refused to look at him.

"I don't love you Joe." She whispered.

"So look at me when you say it," Joe demanded feeling everything that had built up slipping away without reason.

"I don't love you." She looked straight at him. Looking away again she simply sat there staring into space.

Joe didn't know what to do. He sat on the bed next to her. He pulled her towards him to kiss her. She kissed him back all the while saying she shouldn't be there. She needed to get back to her kids. Joe began undressing them both. He wanted to make love to her one last time. He laid her on the bed and she just looked at him. He entered her slowly. "I don't love you," she told him again.

Joe made love to her faster. It was angry love making. She never once told him to stop she just looked to her side moaning in pleasure. Joe wanted to be sure it was what she wanted. He asked her to get on top which she did even though she moaned about her stomach. So she made love to him then before lying back down as Joe entered her again. He was frantic with the movement of his hips. He didn't last long he was crying by the time he had climaxed. He couldn't understand what she was doing.

"Call me a taxi Joe. I have to go back to the kids. It's over we are through." Loren told him as she sat up, getting dressed.

"In a minute. Let's just talk about this."

"No!" Loren screamed at him. She pushed Joe out of her way unlocking the caravan disappearing into the night.

Getting dressed as quickly as he could Joe chased after her. She wasn't anywhere to be seen. He raced up the road to look for her. The road was an open stretch but he couldn't see any sign of her. Eventually he caught up with her wandering around the streets of Kings Norton. He managed to talk her into coming back to the caravan as she phoned her husband. She was telling him that they had had a great night which was spoiled by Joe going crazy. Joe couldn't believe what he was hearing. It had been exactly the opposite. Loren had gone crazy not him. She spoke calmly to her husband on the phone insisting she didn't need him to pick her up as she would be home within the hour. So Joe ordered her a taxi, letting her slip out of his life again. He knew this time it would take a lot of hard work to win her back. He watched her disappear from him again once she got in the taxi, fining himself wondering how much more he could put up with. Loren never seemed to know what she wanted. Joe didn't think he could fix things this time. Closing the caravan door behind him he went to sleep.

The next day at work Joe had a complete breakdown. He did his best to make it through the day only managing to get to lunchtime. His team leader Sally took him in the office telling him it was obvious that he wasn't coping. Sending him home she told him to take the rest of the week off. Joe didn't argue. He felt as though his life had been turned upside down just as things seemed to be going right for a change.

Over the next few weeks Joe was a complete mess. He tried calling Loren, but she eventually changed her mobile number as for her other mobile he could only presume Adrian had taken that from her. He sent her dozens of texts daily for two weeks. He emailed her constantly trying to remind her of the good times. None of it did any good. At one point he got a message from Adrian telling him he was pathetic and that he and his friends were all laughing. This only drove Joe further over the edge. He sent threatening messages to Adrian telling him he would eventually kill him.

This seemed to have an effect as Loren called him the same day.

"What the hell are you playing at? I'm at work and I have had my husband phone me saying you're going to get me, my kids and him. You dare threaten me I will come down there and kill you."

"I have never and will never threaten you or your children," Joe replied calmly. He was being honest. He understood fully what had happened. Adrian had told Loren he had sent him a message saying not just that he had threatened her husband but her entire family. "Ask him to show you a message that says I threatened you or the kids. He can't he is winding you up as he always does. Then you start on phoning me having a go that's what he wants."

"I don't believe you," Loren faltered. The thing was Joe knew she did. He never lied to her where as Adrian always did. She knew that.

"So ask him. Then you can apologise to me."

"Okay I will ask him, and if you're right I will apologise."

"Look I don't want to fight with you Loren. I know you care about me. Maybe it was just all too much for you, but you never gave me any answers."

"You're right Joe it was all too much," she confessed sounding more like her old self. The bitterness she had first greeted him with had all but disappeared from her voice. "And I never said I didn't care. I will think back on our times together with fond memories."

"I still love you," he interrupted.

"I know you do Joe but you will find someone else. Who knows one day we may still be able to meet up as friends, go for a drink if you're not with someone else then."

"Ok," Joe replied. "I'm glad we could end things on a positive note."

"You take care of yourself Joe," replied Loren before hanging up. He never got the chance to say good bye.

So they left it at that. It was a bitter parting for sure, but there could be no other way. The next evening Joe did get an apology. The message from Loren was brief saying she should have known not to believe Adrian but she still wanted nothing more to do with Joe. So after that he got on with his life doing his best to pick up the pieces. It wasn't easy Loren was always in his thoughts. Still as time went on he began to reform a small semblance of life. He didn't think he would ever be the same again.

A few days later his dad knocked on the caravan door. He told him it hurt him to see his son in so much pain. He hadn't seen him in such a bad way since he had been with Katrina when she had aborted his child. He wept in his father's arms then letting it all out.

"You don't understand," he cried, "I love her so much."

"You're stronger than this son. You deserve better. Your problem is you always give too much of yourself. You should never give any woman one hundred per cent the way you do until you are sure they will give it back. If this woman cared anything for you she would be here now."

So Joe cried his tears until he could cry no more in his father's arms, before asking to be left on his own where he cried until he fell asleep. The next morning he woke up pushing Loren to the back of his mind. He concentrated heavily on Ebay when he was at home throwing himself into it like never before. He worked non stop, keeping busy all the while. Another two weeks went by, and slowly the pain began to ease.

Joe eventually calmed down. He hadn't heard from Loren in several weeks. He still thought of her every second that went by, but with that final phone conversation things had ended. He hoped that one day she would get herself sorted. It was something he clung to. He didn't believe she ever would. It was just she had told him, Loren never got around to doing anything. So with Christmas fast approaching Joe did his best to push her out of his life for good. He went on two Christmas works parties. One was basically just for his section of the office at a small Mexican place of the Hagley Road called Chiquitoes. It was a good night, and a fine meal, but when everyone else went on dancing up town Joe just wanted to go home. The next night a week later was for everyone in the building, all teams. It was paid for by the big bosses. It was a meal at the Bushwackers restaurant just by their offices. Mainly it was just a night of boozing for everyone. Joe did his best to forget Loren for that one night. He drank Jack Daniels till it was pouring out of his ears but seemed to stay sober no matter how much he tried to get drunk. Eventually after one of the girls in the office tried it on with him Joe had had enough. He told his mate Larry he was ready to leave. They left heading for the train station. Larry knew all about Joes' on going situation with Loren. He didn't say I told you so or tell him what he thought. Larry just told Joe to do what he thought was right. Joe could only say that he believed he was meant to be with Loren and that one day he would prove it. As far as Joe was concerned it was just a matter of waiting, after all hadn't that always been the case.

Joe had taken Reece to the Christmas pantomime at his parents working man's club. Loren was still all he thought about. He simply couldn't shut her out of his mind no matter how hard he tried even though it had been weeks since he had heard a word from her. The noise on the stage as the pantomime staff set up was doing his head in. The last thing he wanted was to be around people with happy smiling faces making excessive noise. Reece and his cousins all had plenty of pop, as well as sweets. Joe had to leave he couldn't stand to be there. He was no good to his son in the state he was in. Reece wouldn't like it; didn't like it. When Joe tried to leave his son cried his poor little eyes out. How was a child meant to understand? All Reece knew was his daddy wanted to go. Reece would be fine. All his cousins were there as well as Joe's parents to look after him. But try telling that to a four year old. The truth wouldn't wash. So Joe rearranged the seats so that he was sitting behind Reece. He made sure Reece had sweets, crisps and enough pop right next to him so that he wouldn't need to turn his eyes away from the stage. Then when it seemed his attention was away from his father and focused more on the loud booming microphones of the pantomime Joe feeling as guilty as he had ever done with regard to matters of his young son crept away. He felt disgusted with himself.

"It's okay, Joe. You go home it's obvious that you have too much on your mind at the moment. Reece will be fine here with me." His mother had told him before he left.

Joe decided to walk home from Cotteridge. He would be home in twenty minutes. As he walked all he could think about was Loren, it had been weeks since he had heard from her. He wished he could go back in time. There was nothing he could do though. He had no time machine. Such things just didn't exist in the real world. Still even if he could what would he change to make things work, Joe wouldn't have known where to start. He had no idea what really happened between Adrian and Loren that night after he had come back from Salsa with Amanda. He had a good idea that she had told her husband that after the concert she would never see Joe again. It was probably supposed to be their farewell night out in her eyes rather than what Joe thought was the beginning of something new with everything finally out in the open.

Sitting at his PC Joe felt like the walking dead. Try as he might he just couldn't concentrate. He visited the Chatsmart website browsing through the profiles. None of them interested him. He viewed Loren's page, finding himself sitting there for a long time just staring at her picture on screen. He wished he knew how it all went wrong. He could see from the information on the page that she hadn't logged on for days. He just wished she would talk to him.

Then his mobile phone rang, out of the blue.

"It's me I haven't got much credit can you call me back on my mobile?" It was Loren. He couldn't believe it. He had no idea what she wanted. He had sent Adrian some threatening emails a few weeks back, and all that got him was an earful from Loren. He had kept out of her way for weeks.

"What mobile?" he asked confused. Adrian had found out about the mobile she had at work. As far as Joe knew she no longer had it. She had lied to him though hadn't she.

"The number you always call silly."

So with Loren hanging up Joe called her back on the old number. "What?" It was all he could say and his tone was sharp.

"I knew it would be a bad idea to call you."

"Well I'm just a bit surprised. You told me that it was over. I was getting on with my life, or at least trying to. I was at a pantomime with Reece. I couldn't cope so I came home. All I could think of was you." Joe was shaking. Loren always made him shake when she was with him. Now it seemed he only had to hear her voice for it to set him off.

"Look Joe I just thought we could talk again. I'm not promising you anything. You have to understand that. I need to sort myself out. But if you want we can talk again."

"I'd like that. I will be happy with that," Joe told her.

"It's lovely to hear you voice Joe. I have really missed talking to you."

So as they had done so many times in the past the two would be soul mates began chatting again. Joe had volunteered to baby sit Reece at the place he had once called home, Isobel's house in Stechford. Technically it was still half his as his name was still on the deeds, not that he would ever call it home again. So while chatting with Loren he walked back up to Cotteridge to collect Reece and take him back on the bus to Stechford.

"So you still love me, don't you Joe," she said to him at one point. It wasn't a question, more a statement of fact.

"For all my stupid faults Loren, yes I do." He eventually hung up with her telling him to call later. Joe told her that he wouldn't do that but that she could ring at any time and he would call her straight back.

When he eventually got Reece home he managed to find some food in the freezer to do his son some dinner. He made him little chicken dinosaur shapes with chips and beans. Reece didn't finish it all leaving most of it but then Joe hadn't expected him to. His son had more than likely filled his belly that day with unknown amounts of crisps and sweets. He had received a Christmas present at the pantomime from Santa Claus. Joe hadn't been there to stop him opening it, and as all the other children had opened theirs Joe's parents had let Reece open his. He had got a toy electric guitar that had so many different sounds and ways to play it that Joe was pleased. It wasn't just how much enjoyment that Reece would get out of it though. Joe knew full well that Isobel would hate such a gift as Reece would play it non stop doing her head in. He couldn't help grin at that.

When Reece finally went to bed he kept calling downstairs to his dad. "Dad, dad?" he would call.

"Yes Reece?" Joe would answer.

"Love you dad."

"Love you too," He replied. Reece did this three or four times before he eventually fell to sleep. When Joe had been living there it had always been very hard to get Reece to sleep on his own. Joe felt good knowing Isobel was doing a great job bringing up their son.

When Loren called back Joe had to ask her. "Don't you have any work to do tonight?"

"Well you kind of get into the habit of talking again." She said sounding happy.

"I take it you're having a quiet night?"

"Yes well I may have to go into theatre in a moment but I just thought I'd see how you were. Did you and Reece get back ok?"

"Yes I cooked him dinner, and read him a story before putting him to bed. He is asleep now. How are your bunch?"

"They are fine Joe thank you."

"I'm just about to watch when Harry met sally," he told her. "It's a film about soul mates so I think it's very appropriate. Will think of you when I watch it," Joe told her smiling as he put the video in.

"I've never seen it," confessed Loren.

"Well maybe one day we can watch it together."

"Maybe," At that Loren was gone again only for her to repeatedly call Joe time after time that night until her shift ended at nine. It was as if all the time apart had really affected her. Joe knew she had missed him a lot. He also knew he wouldn't be able to keep to his promise of just friends that chat on the phone for very long. He would need to see her again soon. It was Loren that had called him. If all she really wanted was someone to talk to on the phone she wouldn't have got back in touch after everything that had happened between them in the past, of that Joe was positive.

The drinking continued right up until Christmas Eve with everyone finishing work around lunchtime. They all headed for the local pubs once more. Joe just hung around with two or three of his closest friends. They finished their last minute Christmas shopping before finding a few quiet bars. By the end of the afternoon Joe put himself in a Taxi feeling like he could sleep for a week. He got chatting to the black cab driver as he left explaining to the man how expensive it would be for him to pick up his son in a taxi the following day. Taking pity on Joe the man gave him his mobile number telling him to call him, and that he would personally do him a favour as it was Christmas.

"I have no reason to do this," The Asian drive told Joe, "But I can see you want to spend Christmas with your son. I feel sorry for you and will help you. There is nothing in it for me."

Joe accepted the strangers help without hesitation. That was what Christmas was all about, he told himself as he left the taxing driver with a big tip heading to the caravan to sleep off all he had drunk that afternoon.

He slept for several hours waking at nine o'clock. The Jack Daniels he had drunk that afternoon had gone to his head quickly. He awoke feeling rather groggy. Making himself a cup of coffee Joe decided to wrap up the last of Reece's presents. He had left wrapping them until the last minute as he knew with bittersweet certainty he wouldn't be watching his son opening his gifts on Christmas morning that year. Joe would have to wait until the afternoon for that to happen. Still he would call Reece in the morning at least and wish him the best Christmas he could before seeing him later in the afternoon.

He spent an hour or so wrapping his son's presents before deciding he would call it a night. It wasn't like when he was a child, sleep would come easily to him. Joe had long lost the buzz surrounding the festive period that would keep children up at night. He was no longer a child and had long lost any notion of Christmas cheer. He remembered bitterly how one Christmas Eve had had been woken up by his mother arguing with his father. His father was saying how he wouldn't be putting any presents out that year as the kids were all ungrateful. Joe had only been eight at the time, that's when his illusions were shattered. Joe would always remember that morning it was the only time his father didn't get up with everyone else. On that day he hadn't got out of his bed till past eleven in the morning. That year was perhaps one of the worst. He often wondered if his two brothers and his sister had heard his parents that night too.

Sleeping that night proved to be harder than Joe had thought It would be. He kept thinking of Loren. He just wished if he could wish one person some seasonal good will it could be her. So after a good hour or so of tossing around getting tangled in the sheets of his bed Joe left the caravan, and logged onto the PC in the kitchen. A small part of him was saying she will be there. She has to be there. Some things just have to happen. The funny thing was that tiny voice at the back of his head was right. Loren was indeed online.

"Helloooooooooo"

"Merry Christmas," he typed even though it was still only Christmas Eve.

"Merry Christmas Joe."

"I had gone to bed", Joe typed.

"Snap why you up?"

"Thought I'd come on here quickly." Joe typed. Something had told him that Loren would be online to wish him a merry Christmas. She always seemed to be there when it counted the most.

My kids are still up they are so excited. Only Tim's asleep. I'm drinking my wine."

"It's good that we are chatting again."

"Yes but well I can't promise anything just friends, for now at least," she typed back...

"It's funny."

"What's funny?" Loren gave Joe a quizzical if pleasing look.

"I had a hunch you would be online that's all." Joe told her.

"Look it's nearly Xmas five minutes let's wait, then we can shout."

So they waited counting down the minutes as they just sat there in their own respective homes watching each other as they had done on so many occasions in the past, until their computers told them Christmas day was finally upon them and they typed the words together.

"Merry Christmas."

"Can't believe it's Christmas," Joe typed. "I'm glad I got to be the first person to officially say it to you."

"That's why I logged on. I hoped you would be here. Well I have presents still to wrap. Goodnight Joe."

"Night Loren." Joe typed in return before logging off. Christmas had arrived. He has seen it in with the woman he loved. It hurt him that he couldn't spend it with her but was grateful for what little he did have. The next morning he would open up his presents with his family. It would be his first Christmas morning without Reece. It was a time for children. Still Joe would pick Reece up in the afternoon and watch him open his presents then. Joe went to bed with a heavy heart. Life wasn't as bad as it could have been, but it was a long way from as good as it could get.

Christmas evening Joe found himself in his caravan. He had spent the morning drinking in the local working man's club with his family before leaving there to pick up Reece from his mom's. He had been lucky enough to bump into a taxi driver the night before who would give him a lift into Stechford on Christmas day for a cheaper fair than he would normally get. He had explained his situation to the driver after leaving town after a few drinks with some friends Christmas Eve afternoon. The Taxi Driver had felt sorry for Joe and agreed to take him to his son personally. This would be going out of the man's way but Joe was grateful to the stranger for his help. That evening Joe played the game cube with Reece hoping to get a call from Loren at some point. She had told him she would be in work on Christmas day evening for about 4 hours or so. When she did call, Joe even with Reece with him was not too sober.

"How's your day been?" he asked her.

"Terrible," she told him. "I got up watched the kids open their presents. I didn't get anything and all the kids felt sorry for me. Adrian didn't even get me a bloody card."

"You can't really be surprised at that."

"No I know that Joe. Just all day while making the dinner all I have been able to think about is you. I've come in work early just so I can chat to you before I start. You know the one thing I wanted today?"

"what's that?" he asked her.

"A Christmas kiss from you."

Joe could feel his heart melting. His emotions were running high. He would gladly have given her that gift if he could. He knew he had drunk far too much. He couldn't play Sonic the hedgehog very well with Reece for one thing. Still as he talked to Loren now his thoughts were happier ones. He was over the moon to be able to talk to her on this day of all days. So with Reece absorbed in the game cube he continued his chat with Loren.

"So what is it you like about me then Loren? Why me? You keep coming back all the time." He asked her.

"I don't know, erm." She faltered.

"why can't you get me out of your head?"

"I don't know," she repeated. "I mean I have never really had a type that I go for or anything like that. When you were like six years younger than me at first I was like he's six years younger, but that doesn't bother me."

"No it doesn't," Joe said firmly.

"And. I don't know," She faltered again. " I guess you're like me. I like, I like the way you touch me. I don't know. You're just really like me, Joe. We are very very much the same. I feel I can just be me with you. I can just do anything without hiding things when I am with you."

"That's the point. You always can, Loren. You can always be yourself with me and you need to finally realize that and sort yourself out. I really can't keep going on like this with you coming to me one minute, running away the next."

"I understand that, Joe." She pleaded sounding like there was a hint of fear in her voice. "I've said I have to get myself sorted by moving out, finding somewhere to rent big enough for me and the kids."

"You just don't know how close you have continually come to fucking my life up for good. I mean I have never been a suicidal person, but these last few weeks it has crossed my mind. I'd be lying if I said it hadn't" In part that was true. He had thought about it but only in the sense that it was something he would never do even though he wished at the time when Loren had ended things that he wished he could.

"I would have hated you for that," Loren told him.

"There would have been no point in hating me if I was gone he told her."

"I'm just glad we are talking again, Joe I really miss you. I want to see you again soon."

"I would like that too," he told her fearing that in all likely hood what would actually happen would be a one night thing that would lead to more weeks of pain.

So after weeks of silence they were talking once again. Joe got Reece to sing with him down the phone to Loren and all in all they had a good evening. Loren eventually had to return home at nine. After that Joe took Reece into the house just as several relatives were arriving. They had a real family Christmas even if Joe was somewhat worse for wear, with him annoying the hell out of everybody. He could not tell his family about how Loren had gotten back in touch with him. They would certainly hit the roof. So he kept it to himself. He enjoyed the rest of his Christmas night with his son and the rest of his family. He enjoyed spending the better part of boxing day fooling around with Reece playing with his new toys and the game cube. He even went so far as to video all the presents on his mobile to show to Isobel when he took Reece home a few hours later. He was for the time being happier than he had been in a while. He still felt on edge, but had come to accept that as part of his on and off relationship with Loren.

They didn't really talk much over the Christmas period. It wasn't really possible. Loren refused to come online even early in the morning while her kids were still in bed as she had done in the past. Then a few days before New Year's Eve she called him asking him to come up and see her before she started a night shift. She asked him to keep out of sight and meet her at Hope Springs around eight thirty. He would be there she knew he wouldn't say no. She told him she looked forward to being able to give him the kiss she had saved for him since Christmas day.

So it was that Joe found himself once again walking around Hope Springs Hospital. He often wondered if the security at the hospital would ever approach him. He always got there early, spending a good hour walking around before Loren eventually showed up on time just like she always did. It was while walking that a Ford Galaxy drove past him. He knew straight away who it was. It was Loren being dropped off by her husband. She had told him to wait out of sight. Well he had obviously blown that one. Still Adrian didn't seem to notice him at all, but he figured Loren probably nervous as hell must have done. Still he didn't expect Adrian to notice him as he had posted a picture of himself online on Chatsmart with a beard. He had shaved that very evening before leaving knowing full well Loren wouldn't like it. He wanted to kiss her after all. He hadn't seen her in over six weeks. They would kiss it was definite. When she had called him Christmas day she had told him she had gone into work early just so that she could speak to him before she started her short shift. All she wanted to do on that day was share a Christmas kiss with him. Then it was impossible, tonight it wouldn't be. He hid around the corner of one of the Hospital buildings waiting for the Ford Galaxy to drive away. When it did Joe walked around until he found Loren sitting in the dark on one of the many benches that were situated around the various hospital buildings.

She was smoking a cigarette. Seeing him she smiled. "Didn't you see me?" she said blowing out a poof of smoke

"Yes. I saw Adrian too. Surprised he didn't spot me. I can't stop shaking. It's freezing out here, I've been waiting an hour.

"You silly man, Joe."

"I love you," He told her.

"I know you do," she replied. "It is good to see you she said," not giving back his words, "I just get so nervous meeting like this. It always leaves me feeling on edge. I hate it. I told Adrian I was going into work early for a coffee and to watch Eastenders before my shift started."

"So he didn't suspect anything."

"No I think he was glad to be able to get rid of me and go on the pc."

Joe sat beside her smoking one of his own cigarettes holding her hand as he shivered in the cold.

"You scare me half to death woman. I never know what to expect from you. At least I know tonight I'm shaking because I've almost made myself ill waiting in the cold rather than because of how I feel about you."

"You shouldn't be scared Joe, Things will be better once I get my own place," she promised.

They talked for another ten minutes. She told him she didn't have long but was glad he had come up to see her. It was then that they stood up and walked behind the building the bench was beside. She let him press her against the wall as they kissed. Their kisses were strong, passionate, their tongues hungry. Joe had missed her so much. He couldn't stop himself, he found himself touching her breast, squeezing her nipples under her top.

"Joe!" she exclaimed a wicked unbelieving look in her eyes.

Joe was so aroused he couldn't stop. He placed his hands under her skirt, burying them inside her. She moaned with excitement and pleasure. She could hardly protest or make much noise them being them where they were.

"You know what would be better," he groaned feelings her hands upon his stiff member.

She just looked at him and smiled.

"Me inside you," he replied.

"We can't not here," she protested half-heartedly. She wanted Joe then just as much as he did her.

"Just one thrust," he lied. He began to undo his the zip of his trousers moving them down to just enough.

Loren hitched up her skirt guiding him towards her with his hands. "What if someone comes past?" she said obviously not really caring as she kissed him after her question, sighing heavily.

They wrapped their coats around each other as Joe slide inside Loren thrusting himself hard against her; He pushed her body hard against the wall, kissing her neck frantically as he did. She groaned with heavy sighs. He was overcome with excitement. His hips pushed against her the more turned on they both became. He was ready to explode. He couldn't believe what they were doing, doubted Loren could either. He had gone up there to meet her, to talk, to eventually kiss not for this. This was a New Year's Eve he would never forget. He was going to cum he knew it. He held hold off her tightly as he thrust deeper and faster. He knew that it was something he had to do now that he was inside her. He could feel her warmth he wouldn't stop until he had finished what he started. The whole idea of fucking her outside her place of work in the dark when someone could walk past was the biggest turn on of his life. If someone had told him he would be doing what he was at that moment a few hours before he would have laughed at them, even though he had fantasised about doing exactly what he was the night before. That's all it should have been, just a fantasy, these kinds of things just didn't happen he told himself as he felt himself reaching that crucial moment. Joe held onto Loren tightly, not saying a word, fearing that if she knew he was about to orgasm that she would pull away from him, not that she could with her body pressed tightly against the wall her one legged wrapped around his waist. From the sounds she was making he wondered if she cared about anything other than what they were doing at that time. He doubted her mind could be thinking of anything other than Joe being inside her, fucking her against the wall. Then he exploded, his body went limp, his cock stayed hard, Joe sighed at the bitter end of it. It was over and she would now leave him and go back to work.

"I've cum," he smiled at her. Joe couldn't stop the biggest grin of his life spreading across his face. This really was a happy new year.

"You haven't," she said with mock surprise.

"I have."

"You just want to get me pregnant," she laughed kissing him gently.

"So what if I do, Ice," he replied using the new nickname he had given her a short time ago. "I have never made any secret of it you are a great."

"And you would make a great father for my child, Joe," she told him. "It's hardly very good circumstances to be letting something like that happen. Now I really have to go. I know you never want me to but what with you fucking me I'm going to be late now."

She left then walking away without looking back.

"Ice," he called out and was at her side in an instant pulling her close.

Loren kissed him one more time. "Look go."

I'll speak to you later when I can. Just go Joe. It's been wonderful seeing you."

So Joe made his long journey home back to his caravan. It took him over two hours and several buses. It wasn't easy as the timetables had all changed what with it being New Year's Eve. He called Larry who had always been a good ear to him regarding his problems with Loren. He told his friend almost everything, leaving out the goodbye fuck that they had shared. That was what it was. They hadn't made love that time. Making love wasn't something you did against a wall in the dark. They had simply missed each other so much that they had become overcome with lust. Still Joe couldn't have imagined the night going any better.

When Joe arrived back home it was going on eleven. He had tried calling Loren during that time but got no answer other than a short text telling him she was busy in theatre and that Hope Springs was simply manic.

"I can't believe you fucked me, Joe," was the first thing she said when she did answer the phone, having gotten a short cigarette break around eleven thirty. "I walked into work thinking my god I've just been fucked." She laughed at this.

"Well it was good to know you wanted me and it was great knowing we were both sober so we both wanted it." he told her.

"Yes I know."

"So really busy tonight,"

"very much but I'll call you just after midnight to wish you a happy year I promise you that. I can't call straight away as the kids will want to speak to me."

"And Adrian," Joe added.

"Yes and my husband." She admitted. "We have been together a long time there will always be something between us. Even when we do go our separate ways I'd like to think we can become better friends when all this is sorted, and I have my own place."

"When do you think that will be?"

"I don't know," Loren sighed. It was obvious by the sound in her voice that she really didn't know. Joe knew full well she hated the pressure he put on her to move out. The thing with Joe was he also knew that Loren would never get around to doing anything to change her situation unless she was given a little push now and then. It had always been the way with them. They would break up with Loren saying it was all getting too much, that she need space, only for them to get back together a few weeks later with Loren admitting to how much she missed him, how she knew he was right. I'm going to get myself sorted was something he always heard from Loren. He thought perhaps he had heard her say that one too many times.

So they saw the new year in together. Joe called Reece quickly, knowing Isobel would keep him up. You could always see fireworks from the house in Stechford as the new year came about. Reece would be up watching them. He wished his son a happy new year, moments later speaking to Loren telling her he hoped things would finally work out between them. She agreed with him completely telling him not to worry and that she would sort herself out soon and he would be mighty surprised.

The funny thing is Jo should have learnt his lesson with Loren by then. The one thing she always said about herself was that she never got around to doing anything. So did she find a place to live? No. Did she feel guilty for the time they had shared outside the hospital that New Year's Eve? That was Loren's way one minute she would say she wanted a quiet life bury herself in work and the kids, the next she would come running to Joe for a crazy night out.

Things were different though what with their days of internet chatting long gone, so was a part of their relationship. The concert had been a magical night marred by Loren's self-destructive nature.

It was a couple of weeks later they arranged another date to see each other. This time it would be an evening in the caravan.

Things went just as they normally would that night, with Loren turning up in a taxi, Joe paying and them having a wild night fuelled with drink and lovemaking. Joe didn't think she would show up. Joe couldn't shake the nagging thought that sooner or later she would let him down. After what had happened that night at the Darren Hayes Concert when Loren had flipped out he just expected her to eventually do it again. Sure their relationship was very rocky due to her still living with Adrian, but whenever they were together they seemed to have the time of their lives. They talked all night in between making love. Joe was happy to know that Loren had finally agreed to accept his offer of a loan. She told him it would be easier for him to browse the internet for properties that she could afford. It made sense. The more she seemed to want leave home the more pressure she would get from Adrian, who for all his crimes still loved his wife. So Joe had started looking. He went to a few different website and signed up so that new properties to Loren's liking would be emailed to him as soon as they became available. It wasn't easy. Not only did Loren want something affordable which was obvious, but she wanted a large house for the kids, as well as something that was close to Hope Springs, and the school. She wanted the gingerbread house in a way. Loren wanted the best. For all the woman's talk of not being materialistic in the slightest she was probably the most materialist woman Joe had ever met. That night he didn't let it worry him. He had bought a checkers board for them to play. He had bought a deck of cards. They tried to play checkers. It didn't work. It just wasn't the same as the old days when they had chatted online and used the game as an excuse. Joe just thought it would have been fun to really play checkers even though all he could think of was making love to her. Then the cards came out. Loren spent a good half hour just shuffling them as she talked to Joe about her life. She told him about the agony of losing her mom. How the pair of them used to go out together, to play bingo and get drunk. She told him of a time when she was younger when an old man who owned a house at the bottom of her garden, a family friend as is usually sadly the case, who had eventually raped her when she was just a little girl. She told Joe that if she ever met the guy again now that she was an adult she would have no hesitation in killing him whether that meant prison or not. Joe could understand why. Hearing the tale himself for the first time upset him, made him feel like killing the guy too, if indeed he was still alive. Every time he got to spend some quality time with Loren it seemed she had a new tale of anguish from her past to share with him. Eventually their need for each other overcame the talk. The troubles of the past were soon forgotten as their passion was ignited. They did some crazy things that night. It was to be expected every night they spent together seemed to have a crazy moment or two. At one point she raced out of the caravan naked leading Joe god knows where. Only to say to him where are we going Joe? Joe simply rested her body against a tree taking her there and then. Upon returning to the caravan it was Loren who told Joe what would really turn her on would be for him to take her in his parent's house, which he did, making love to her yet again on the living room floor of his parent's house. No one ever knew. The only comment he got the next morning was from his father who asked him what on earth his clothes had been doing in the middle of the living room floor. Joe could only shrug his shoulders and say that he had no idea as he had been drunk. His parents had no idea he was seeing Loren again. He couldn't tell them.

A week later while talking on the phone they agreed the next night they spent together would be a night at a hotel so they could spend some proper quality time together not having to worry about Joe's parents or anyone else. It would be hard, but Loren told Joe she would simply fake a night shift at Hope Springs. She would tell Adrian that work had asked her to work an extra shift and that as she was saving to move out would need the extra money.

So two weeks later Joe booked a hotel. They didn't chat on the internet anymore like the old days. Talking while Loren was working was always touch and go. If she was on an early shift Joe would leave home at seven to start work in Birmingham city centre at nine, spending two hours trying to get through. It made him so anxious. He wondered if things would ever be different. He spent the rest of the week wondering how much longer Loren would tell him the old lie of I will get myself sorted, until the Saturday that he had booked them into the hotel came around.

How many times had Joe done what he was doing? He waited in the dark of Hope Springs on a cold Saturday night. Normally this would mean he was meeting Loren for a brief half hour before work. This time he was keeping well out of the way on the other side of the hospital, the accident and emergency ward. It had been Loren's idea for them to spend a night in a hotel. She told him she loved spending time with him and while the caravan was nice it would be good for them to spend a proper romantic evening together. Their texts that they had been sending each other on the build up to that night had been very intimate if not downright sordid. They messaged each other the things they wanted to do with each other that night. She had told Adrian that she was working a night shift which meant her and Joe would actually be able to spend the night together with her not having to leave until six thirty the following morning. Joe had booked them into a hotel near Hope Springs called the Wychbold for the night. This was a first for them. A real intimate evening with a comfy bed rather than the makeshift but bearable one he slept in every night in his caravan.

    Over his shoulder he carried his rucksack filled with everything Loren had asked him to bring. There was a Walkman in there with a small supply of batteries, as well as some small speakers to go with it. Loren loved her music. Joe couldn't imagine a night with Loren without some form of music in the background. The Walkman and its tiny speakers wouldn't be loud but it was better than nothing. He had also bought a bottle of wine, as well as some coke he had only moments before bought from a local late night store in Sutton Coldfield. As usual he had gotten there far too early so had plenty of time. He had deliberately left buying the bottle of coke till the last minute not wanting the rucksack to be too heavy on his way to Sutton. He had also brought with him two other things, a pot of strawberry yoghurt for fun with Loren, something he had always fantasised about and was eager to try that night. Lastly he had a single red rose. He hadn't thought about buying her flowers until he had arrived in Birmingham city centre. When he got there he had seen a man selling the roses and decided it would be the final touch to start their romantic evening of passion off.

She appeared as if from nowhere. Joe had been keeping an eye out his stomach doing summersaults as it always did as he waited for her. As soon as he saw her smiling face her eyes shining like the very meaning of life his stomach calmed down, the butterflies subsided. It was as though whenever she was around him all was right in the world.

"Didn't think you'd show up," he told her.

"I always do."

"I know but I always think one day you won't come."

"Well I've never let you down yet and if ever I couldn't get out you know I'd let you know."

Her words were true enough and as they called a taxi to take them to the hotel that awaited them she told him how Adrian had been going against her wishes and got the children a dog. It was bad enough with things at home as they were she told him seeming a bit frustrated. Now she had what seemed like an even larger family to cope with.

Joe didn't like the idea of them having a pet. It just made the whole setup even more bizarre. It was as though she was still doing nothing. Okay so Adrian had gotten the dog against her wishes but the way Joe could see it was that there was a family, a husband and wife with children, with now the added bonus of a dog. It was a real perfect setting to anyone looking in from the outside.

When they eventually arrived at the Wychbold they found that someone was celebrating their Birthday. In the hotels bar which extended to a fairly good sized dance floor with tables of food running alongside it, were a large number of people. They were all apparently there to give their best wishes to someone known only as Bill to the two lovers who were unintentionally gate crashing this little party.

After unpacking upstairs they sat and talked while drinking wine as Joe's Walkman played quietly in the background.

Loren had brought a tape full of all her favourite songs which now played in the Walkman. She rejoiced in telling Joe how a lot of the songs on there reminded her of her mother. A few of them she insisted even reminded her of Joe.

Joe sat watching her from the double bed. She was beautiful regardless of the fact she could never wear makeup when with him. She was one of the few women he had ever met that had a natural beauty about them. She eventually came to lie beside him, snuggling up to him as she lay on her side.

"Why me?" Loren had repeatedly asked him the same question on numerous occasions before. She knew the answer as well as he.

"Because I love you barmy lady," he sighed as he moved close so that he could kiss her. Lifting over her top he dropped it lightly to the floor, before unbuttoning her bra throwing it to the same place as her top as he kissed her upper body.

Loren moaned with delight at his touch. She laid her head back on the pillow staring into his eyes. "Turn off the lights," she told him as she pulled down her jeans.

Joe did as she asked pitching them into darkness. He loved looking at her naked body, but could understand the way she felt. His eyes would soon adjust to the dark. He undressed himself as he continued to kiss her whole body working his way from her neck to her inner thighs. He kissed her in her most intimate area making her moans and sighs deepen as the pleasure he gave her soared with every passing minute. He used his fingers as well as his tongue and licked and sucked at her insides until her entire body was going into spasms of pleasure.

"Make love to me Joe," she whispered softly.

He worked his way back up her body letting his kisses linger on her stomach, the stretch marks she hated so much. He loved every inch of her he didn't share any of her concerns. She was the first woman he had ever had any true feelings for. There was no need for her to worry with him he loved her for who she was not what she looked like. Lying on top of her he entered her slowly looking straight into her eyes as his hips met hers, as they began to make love for what wouldn't be the only time that night. Their lovemaking went on for over an hour as they moved their bodies all over the bed. They moved like one as they entangled each other into positions that gave them greater pleasure until both were satisfied. They lay there in the dark after just staring at one another for a long time. Joe loved Loren with all his heart. He was thankful to be able to spend such an intimate moment with her. It wasn't like the first night. That night had been very special for them both. This night was about exploration, about them opening up to each other sexually. The night had only just begun.

They shared a cigarette then taking a break from the fun of intimate moments that would follow. Joe poured them both more wine as he sat crossed legged on the bed before her gazing at her naked body.

Noticing his stairs Loren did as she always did. Covering her midriff with the bedclothes as her insecurities got the better of her. Joe knew that later when she was more comfortable that would not happen.

"It's funny the amount of times we have been together we never use anything. I would have thought you would have been pregnant by now. I have a good mind to get myself tested at a clinic. I'm seriously worried I may be sterile.

"Look stop a minute. Just sit with me I need to tell you something."

"Okay what you going to tell me it's over again?"

"No look there's a good reason why I have never got pregnant with you in the past."

"And what's that?"

"No it doesn't matter. Look let's not ruin the night just make love to me Joe. We don't need to use anything now. Just fuck me."

Joe went to protest. She hushed him with her fingers to his lips as she pulled him on top of her. "I want to see the look on your face when you cum inside me," she told him. Then he was inside her making love to her like he had so many times before only with a harder brutality to it. "Fuck me. Joe fuck me hard." And Joe did. He pulled at her hair holding it tight in his grasp with every thrust. It was the wildest sex they had ever had. Earlier that night they had talked about sex. Joe had asked how he was different from Adrian even though she was adamant they hadn't had sex in years. She told him there was no intimacy between her and Adrian. She also said there were two types of sex Lovemaking and straight fucking. She liked that her and Joe did both.

"Look at me she said tightening her muscles around him as he moved inside her. He was overcome with excitement for her. Her words ignited his body like nothing else. It wasn't long before the pair of them climaxed together with Loren staring deep into his eyes as she felt him deep inside her. The thing with making love to Loren was even after he had an orgasm he wasn't finished. It was weird but he just didn't wilt he carried on as though he could orgasm all night which in the past he had done. This time Loren pulled away moving to his side.

"The reason I haven't got pregnant with you, Joe," she began to tell him sheepishly. "Well it's that I have always taken the morning after pill. If I hadn't I'd be pregnant by now and that wouldn't be right."

Joe sat up shocked at what he was hearing. He didn't like it one bit. She could have at least been honest with him. It always seemed to be one lie after the next with Loren. He had gotten used to her lies by now of course. "Why didn't you tell me before?"

"Because you wanted to get me pregnant." She was unable to stop her laughing as she said it. For some reason the idea of Joe getting her pregnant or the fact he wanted to always amused her. I didn't want to hurt you," she conceded " it might not matter now. The last time I tried to take the pill I didn't take it till way after forty eight hours. Adrian saw me coming out of the doctors and I couldn't get the prescription in time. He asked me what I was doing and I had to lie and say that I had an upset stomach. So he drove me home and I was late getting the pill. I did eventually take it but I've been feeling really sick of late. I think I may be pregnant, Joe."

Joe couldn't help but smile. That's why she didn't bother asking him to use protection that night like they had planned. He had brought some with him like she asked but he hadn't bothered wearing anything. Now he knew why she hadn't asked him. Still he didn't like the lies. If she had just told him to use some protection from the start then she would never have needed to be so secretive with him. He felt like her taking the pill behind his back was another way of having a quick abortion. It was absurd of him to think like that. After what Katrina had put him through nearly seven years earlier he couldn't see it any other way. He hated the idea of the morning after pill. If

Loren hadn't wanted to use condoms then why didn't she go on some form of contraceptive? Joe had always heard bad rumours about the morning after pill like the idea that it made the chances of a woman getting pregnant in the future less possible, and he knew from women he had talked to in the past that it made you incredibly Ill. It answered something else Joe thought. Perhaps the reason Loren was always so cranky the day after their nights out wasn't down to her drinking but rather the fact that she always took the morning after pill. It was Joe thought a plausible explanation for her constant mood swings.

"I guess I've been feeling really broody lately. At first I was like god no. But I know the kids; especially Harriet would be okay with it. They would love another brother or sister." She told him, not noticing the look of sadness on his face at what he was hearing until she had finished. She came towards him then holding him as she kissed his forehead lightly. Joe figured that she must have known the damage she had done by telling him. At least she had been honest enough to finally tell what she had been doing, perhaps that was a start.

"How do you really feel about me Loren?" he asked as she climbed on top of him sliding him inside her with a mischievous grin.

"Well I'm hoping you will eventually be my next husband she said as she moved her hips upon him as they began to make love for the second time that night.

Joe moved forwards smiling. He met his lips with hers as they made love slowly. Neither of them finished that time. After ten or twenty minutes of exploring every inch of each other Joe told her to get dressed. They were going to go and join the party downstairs, have themselves a little dance. They would have plenty of time for love making later. At this idea Loren's face lit up. The woman loved to dance.

So they both got dressed. Loren put her skirt back on and that brown short sleeved jumper she always seemed to wear and they made for the door.

"What do you see in me?" he asked.

"Shut up, Joe," she scolded him;" you know I love you."

"Don't say that," he told her angrily. "You can't take it back. Let's just pretend you never said it. You know full well you don't mean it."

They would have had a blazing row then. Loren had that same fire in her eyes that meant see was about to flip. Joe pressed her body against the door kissed her, he entered her despite the fact that she was clothed fucking her hard against the door. "Let's dance," he told her.

"Okay then Joe," she smiled with a laugh," But you need to stop fucking me."

So they danced. At first they asked the hotel staff if anyone would mind if they gate crashed the private party. The barman they had spoken to just shrugged telling them no one would pay them any attention as long as they kept themselves to themselves. They took to the dance floor. Joe was a pretty crappy dancer. Still it didn't matter. Loren didn't mind she loved dancing and seemed to love dancing with Joe even more. She requested a song for Joe, one of his favourites from his childhood; Come on Eileen by Dexie's Midnight Runners. They screamed the song at each other as they danced, stamping their feet at the appropriate moments. They were having yet another mad night.

They had several drinks down stairs in the bar. Before eleven thirty came to pass and all the lights suddenly turned on. The music stopped signalling the end of the party they had inadvertently joined. Still they had enjoyed a good hour or so of dancing, it was turning out to be one of the best night they had ever had, and Joe still had his pot of yoghurt.

So with no other option they went back up to the room. They continued to make love that Saturday for another five, or six hours, maybe more. Though really making love wasn't exactly what they were doing that night. They were simply having fun exploring each other's sexual desires. Joe did indeed use his yoghurt pouring it all over her and licking it off every single inch he could. It was his ultimate fantasy and he had been allowed to do it with the woman he cared most for in the world. He took her in the shower, against the hotel door, even outside the room where she insisted he cum again so that she could see that ever so content look upon his face. That didn't stop them. They nearly had another argument purely because Joe was fighting his tiredness. Loren let him sleep. He only drifted off for half an hour, not that he knew he had for several weeks later. By the time it came to the early hours of the morning the room was trashed. During one moment of passion they had lay upon the hotel floor having frantic sex. The wine glasses they drank had been smashed to the floor, the bed they had made love on, explored each other on had been kicked to the other side of the room by Joe as he thrust inside his love. Even when it came time for Loren to leave they were still at it both fully clothed lying on the floor still making love. In the end Joe had to admit defeat and order her a Taxi. They handed in their room key and waited outside. There wasn't much else for them to say to each other. They were shattered. Loren would probably be aching and bruised for weeks. They had never made love so passionately or furiously in all their time together.

"Thank you for a wonderful night, Joe," she smiled kissing him lightly.

"I just hope it's not too long before the next time," he smiled returning her kisses as he wrapped her in his arms until the taxi finally showed.

A few weeks later they spent another night at that same hotel. That time there was no private party to crash as it was on a week night. Still they had their room. They had several bottles of wine, and most importantly of all they had each other. So once again they had a mad crazy night of lovemaking. They talked for hours as they always did. Everything seemed to be finally going their way. All they needed was a little more time, and a good enough property to turn up so that Loren could move out.

He hadn't expected to see Loren for a while after that night. She couldn't keep telling Adrian she was working an extra shift. They both knew that he only needed to take one look at her payslips and he would see she had been lying all along. So when two days later on a night, on the Monday she wasn't working he got a call from her out of the blue Joe was gob smacked. Adrian had returned home from some woman's house he had spent the Saturday night with. He had disappeared while she had slept off her supposed night shift duty. He hadn't told their kids exactly where he was going, not returning until over a day later. Loren had told the kids that their father would be home any minute but he had stayed out the entire night without even a phone call. At least with her the kids always came first. Apparently he had only been speaking to the woman for a few days online. This made Loren furious. After everything she had been through with Joe how could Adrian be so two faced. He had always insisted she didn't do anything while they live under the same roof, yet as soon as he caught someone's attention he had jumped at the chance. It kicked off a huge argument as Loren drank her weekly bottle of wine. It was one rule she told Joe she always stuck to. Once a week she made a promise to herself that no matter what her husband said about her drinking, not matter how much he protested against it, she bought herself a bottle of wine. Adrian had mentioned to Joe how he thought his wife was nothing but a slag for sleeping with him. Loren had been angry at that explaining to her other half that what had happened between her and Joe had been between two people that deeply cared about each other. When they had made love for the first time it was after a very long courtship between two people. The argument eventually got physical with Loren telling Adrian that if he so much as laid a finger on her she would call the police. It was then that she had left the house explaining to her kids she was going out drinking at the local social club for the night. What she had actually done was find herself a taxi and head straight for Joe. Joe was always there for her, always would be. So that was the story she told Joe. He listened in silence not sure of how much to believe. So much of what Loren told him always seemed to be half-truths. She was on her way and maybe just maybe now that she had stood her ground things would get better. Joe found that he had thought that same thing to himself too many times before.

So she had come to him yet again for another night. They made love as they always did while listening to music and drinking plenty of lager. Joe knew he would have to make sure Loren got home safely that night. She told Joe she had had enough Of Adrian. If he could go out without telling her, do what the hell he liked, then from now on she would do the same. Joe tested her on that by asking her to come out for a meal with him the following week. If she meant what she said then she would have no problem with that. She agreed without any hesitation saying it would be lovely to sit down with Joe on a proper date. It was just another crazy night for the couple.

She had brought various photographs with her fearing that in the aftermath of her argument with Adrian he would lose it, tear them up, or burn them. She showed him a picture of Harriet. When Joe had last seen Loren's daughter on the webcam she had dark brown hair, In the photograph Loren held Harriet had blonde hair, apparently it had been taken several years before.

"What colours her hair now?" Joe found himself asking.

"Blond like in this picture." Loren told him. "Harriet changes her hair almost as much as me." Loren smiled.

"I do miss them you know, the kids. In the beginning I used to see them all the time when we chatted online. I know I never actually met them but I grew really close to them." Joe sighed.

"I'm sure you will meet them one day. They are a handful though. You don't know what your letting yourself in for with my lot. You wouldn't cope."

There were other pictures. One was of Loren's father. Her real father not her step dad who had brought her up. Her real father had left when she was younger. He had been an abusive man Loren told Joe. If she ever saw him again she would kill him. She didn't know why she carried that picture around she just did.

Then she showed Joe a picture of her singing at a karaoke with her mom. She loved her mom and missed her a great deal. Joe couldn't even begin to understand the pain Loren must have felt each and every day. His own mother was still alive. The biggest fear he had was losing her.

The last picture was one of her husband, Adrian which she laughingly told Joe he obviously didn't want to see before she put the collection of photographs back in her bag.

They stayed in the caravan at least, not wandering off for any crazy sexual shenanigans in the dark as they had done in the past. They just spent the night enjoying each other's company as they listened to music; made love, and talked till the early hours of the morning. They made love that night to a song Joe found was one of his favourites from Maroon 5. It was called Sunday Morning. That first night of the hotel they had been true to the song and woke up together on a Sunday morning. It would be nice if one day when they woke neither of them had to rush off. Joe figured he would stick around until that time came. So when two thirty came Joe poured Loren a glass of coke, asking her to get dressed, and ordered her a Taxi to take her back to her husband. It wasn't what he wanted, but he knew full well he couldn't hassle her. If he wanted things to ever get better between them he needed to let the two married people in his life end their relationship on their own. Kissing her farewell he didn't follow her out of the caravan when her taxi arrived he simply told her to take care. She replied with her usual comments of how lovely and nice Joe was before disappearing in the night with a promise on her lips that they would definitely be having a meal the following week.

    They started the evening off at a restaurant on Broad Street. It was a southern American style place called Old Orleans. The lighting was of the dimly lit variety that gave the place a gloomy feel rather than the ambient nostalgic flavour it hoped to bestow on its visitors. Still it must have been doing something right as the place was packed. Joe had been there years before, not for a meal but the fantastic cocktails they did such as the flaming Lamborghini, a cocktail that was set alight then quickly put out before you drank it. They had to wait a good fifteen minutes to get a table so Joe ordered them a few spirits from the bar. Loren was on double vodka's with orange juice as usual while he just drank a coke. It was their first real date in ages. He wanted to keep as sober as he could, not let his emotions run too high, so that he could just enjoy the time he had with her.

While they waited Loren spotted a leggy blonde enter the bar with her boyfriend.

"I saw you looking," she told Joe with a big grin across her face. "It's ok I don't get jealous over things like that."

Joe was a bit puzzled. He hadn't noticed the blonde with far reaching legs until Loren had pointed her out. The woman was definitely very attractive.

"Excuse me?"

"That woman with the legs," she repeated "Don't tell me you didn't see her."

Joe laughed at that. He had actually had a bit of a stiff neck. When he was supposed to have seen the woman in question he had been stretching his neck to alleviate the cramp he felt. This Loren had obviously seen presuming Joe was eyeing up the woman. "To be honest no I hadn't if I had I would most certainly have taken a look. I'm only human, but as it is I'm with you, and ever since I have been with you I haven't had any real interest in anyone else. It amused Joe no end when the woman and her man sat right opposite them making Loren go unusually quiet. Luckily for them their table was ready by then. Joe pulled back Loren's chair watching her sit down at the table before taking the seat opposite.

They ordered some more drinks while they looked at them menu. Joe had decided it wouldn't hurt to move back to his trusted pal Jack Daniels for the time being. He wasn't all that hungry, but said nothing to Loren. He had been snacking all day. It wasn't that he had been that hungry during the day it was just that when he was at work he always got bored, and seemed to find comfort in food, besides whatever the junk he ate was doing to his body. He never put any weight on not even on his stomach.

 They eventually had a lovely meal with a starter that consisted of breadcrumb mushrooms. They came with mayonnaise and a spicy dip that neither of them recognised. By the time the starter was done with Joe wasn't really all that hungry at all, what with his snack intake throughout the day. He had wanted to order swordfish which he had never had in his life. Joe always liked to try new things when he was out for a meal. This little idea was put straight out of his head when Loren told him she wouldn't be kissing on that night if he had fishy breath. So instead he eventually had the same as her a chicken breast covered in a rich cheese surrounding by lots of vegetables. The thing was as nice as the idea of a meal was the food just wasn't what they liked. They were two people who loved their Sunday roast or even a bowl of pasta, not some fancy American style dishes. Joe was too nervous to eat at any rate. He always had butterflies when he was in Loren's company.

 "You know what I was thinking just," he said on returning from a break to the men's room. He sat back down into his chair waiting for her response to his question

"I'm not fucking you in the toilets so don't even think it," she replied as she ate her meal.

"No," laughed Joe wondering if the woman realised how much he cared for her. That had been the last thing on his mind even though if she had asked him to take her there and then he would have had no problem clearing the table and doing just that. Sometimes he felt as though their relationship was based for the most part on sex. Of late that's what it had become, but then they rarely got any time together so it wasn't surprising they were intimate whenever they got the chance.

"No I was thinking how nice it is to be on a proper date for a change. We have never done anything like this in all the time we have been together. Well except for maybe that time when we first went out to the karaoke. But this is the first sit down meal we have had together."

"Fun isn't it?" she smiled.

"But what do you think of the food really?" he asked giving her a knowing look.

"It's great," she told him before adding. "But I do prefer my Sunday roast."

"I know what you mean," Joe smiled.

They left soon after. They hadn't finished their meals. The vegetables had been too undercooked for their liking. Joe and his lady preferred vegetables to be boiled until all the goodness was out of them so that they were nice and mushy. Paying for the meal with his credit card,

Joe walked out of Old Orleans Loren's hand in his. He felt good to be out in the open. He had felt stuffy sitting down at the table; he was glad that they were on the movie

"So where are we going to dance?" he asked. Joe didn't care where they went as long as they were together. The night was going well despite the meal neither of them had enjoyed.

"Reflex," she said simply. It was the eighties bar they had been too drunk to get into on their first real night out together so many months ago.

This time they entered Reflex without a problem. There was no one at the door to stop them entering it was still early. There was also the fact that they weren't bringing drinks they had brought from another bar in with them this time. The place was pretty empty. Joe knew it would fill up later that night. Thursday was the new Friday night so the local radio station DJ was often heard saying. Still they ordered themselves some drinks, Loren paying this time. Loren had rarely if ever paid for anything on their nights out, not that Joe ever held that against her. Their meetings had always been very secretive and explaining where the money went to her husband would always be a problem

Taking their drinks they walked around the bar standing close the DJ booth. Next to the booth was a small circular disc, rotating over the floor at the side of the main dance floor.

Loren placed her bag on the floor just behind the dance floor using Joe's leather jacket to hide it from any would be bag snatchers that would easily be able to take it once the place filled up. They started to dance with Loren leading Joe to the revolving part of the dance floor.

As the night went on Reflex slowly filled up with people until it was crammed. Joe would occasionally go to the bar to get them more drinks only to find some guy or other chatting up Loren asking for her phone number. Loren told each one in turn they could dance where they wanted but she was there with her boyfriend. She had no interest in anyone else. It made Joe feel good to know that she didn't care for the attention of these other men. Still his jealously was only a normal human emotion and he found himself testing her by taking frequent breaks to the men's room to see how she would cope with her would be admirers. They requested so many songs that night from Footloose to Come on Eileen. They were Joe's favourites.

There was one guy in particular that got to Joe that night. A bald head man with a moustache who seemed to think he was the life and soul of the party. He was in many ways an exaggerated caricature Of Loren's personality. He had great confidence, chatting up every woman he saw in the place. So it was no surprise to Joe when he turned his attentions to Loren. At one point he bought Loren a drink. Rather than take it Loren told Joe it was for him. Joe loved Jack Daniels and had no problem taking the guys money even if the drink was fuelling his jealously. At one point when Joe had disappeared to get them both more drink Mr Moustache even asked Loren to meet him the day after for some fun. Loren had just laughed in his face telling him he had no chance. Well that's what she had told Joe anyway. It had to be the truth didn't it or why would she bother to tell him about the incident at all? The thing is it placed a seed of doubt in Joe's mind. He tried to ignore it as best he could. He began to dance with Loren closer than he had during that night. He kissed her passionately, bending her over railings, pushing her body against the walls. She loved it all of course she did, but did she realise how hurt he was feeling seeing all the attention she was getting. It wasn't her fault of course she was an amazingly attractive woman. That night made Joe realize how hard it would be for him in the future. Still he had to trust her or there would never be anything between them.

So for the rest of that night they danced. Joe pushed Mr Moustache man out of his head. Eventually the guy who wanted Loren to meet him the day after left. Joe searched the entire bar for him fearing he would come back to try his luck again. He never did and Joe was grateful. Loren could handle any trouble. Joe knew that. It just pained him to see so many men approach her looking for a bit of fun.

In the end the lights came on, the music stopped, all the dancing for that evening was done. They walked slowly down Broad Street arm in arm. Loren wanted to get a taxi there and then. Joe insisted they walk to the taxi rank at the station which caused them to have a small argument.

"You're just upset because you didn't get any tonight." She told him.

"No," Joe told her. He didn't want to argue. He had really enjoyed the evening despite the guy with the moustache winding him up. "I don't want you. Well no I always want you, but I enjoyed having a night out dancing. I just wanted us to walk together for a bit so that you just didn't disappear straight after the club. You know I always miss you when you gone, and get upset when you leave."

By then they had reached the escalators that led them down into New Street station and the awaiting line of taxis

"Okay Joe. I'm sorry."

"We could go somewhere else to dance if you like?" Joe suggested.

"No I promised the kids," Loren told him after giving the idea some thought. "Besides you have spent enough money tonight.

She pulled him close letting him feel the warmth of her body against his.

"I love you," he told her.

"I know you do," came her usual reply. Why did she always have to be so cold?

They kissed a bittersweet farewell as Loren got into a taxi as she always did leaving Joe standing alone in the dark. He wondered when he would next see her.

Loren had told Joe that she would see him every week where possible, but over the next few weeks one thing after another came up. First it was Harriet's Birthday so Loren needed all her money for that. She could hardly make any excuses to Adrian that week as she was working two late shifts as well. So Joe didn't argue that time knowing the kids would always have to come first. She insisted she would see him the week after only to say she had made plans to go out on a Hen night with friends. This Joe didn't like one bit. He admitted to her he was jealous but that wasn't really it. If they had been a proper couple Joe would have had no problem with Loren going to the Hen night. The fact was they rarely spent any time together, even though they had been spending more time together recently. Joe just felt as though she was pushing him away. Whenever she was at work she always seemed too busy to call him. He would speak to her for half an hour maximum when he would have spoken to her for several hours in the past.

So several weeks went by with Joe growing even more agitated at the fact he was back to seeing his supposed girlfriend once in a blue moon just when she had told him things would start to get better. He didn't like arguing with Loren but he had been putting his life on hold for far too long without Loren seeming to do a thing. She was still in exactly the same position she had been in when they met. She was still living at home with her husband with no real way out. All Joe ever heard from her was that she needed to get her life sorted. The thing that ached Joe's heart the most was that Loren didn't seem to have a clue as to how she would actually accomplish what she told him she needed to do. Loren seemed content to carry on with the way things were seeing Joe whenever she felt like it.

The following weekend Joe had Reece overnight. Loren was on a night shift but he waited until he got a few texts from her before calling.

"So how are things?" he asked.

"Things are quiet at work," Loren answered knowing full well that wasn't what Joe was asking.

"So how are things at home?"

"Everything's fine." Loren said

"So still no closer to moving out, or getting a loan from a bank or anything."

"I don't want to argue Joe."

"Me neither, but we wouldn't have these kind of conversations if you actually got off your arse and did something." Joe told her his anger rising. He didn't want to fight with her, but felt like she was pushing him into one by doing nothing all the time. He had to make her see that he couldn't hang around forever while she didn't seem to be making any headway.

"I know."

"You know I could lend you the money. You then wouldn't have any excuse you could get a place and sort yourself out."

"I won't take your money, Joe, You know that."

"What if it's the only option?"

"I will cross that bridge when we come to it. Anyway what have you got planned for Reece?" Loren asked Joe as she changed the subject.

Joe didn't see any reason to continue that particular line of conversation she would only tell him things he had heard before. It wasn't the first time he had offered to help her out financially. The response would always be the same. As far as Joe was concerned it was the only way out Loren really had. There was no way she would ever get a loan from a bank the woman was just too heavily in debt.

"I'm just going to take him home. Do him some dinner, and watch some cartoons. We are going to Cotteridge first to look at some charity shops. My mom's told me I might be able to get some good deals on books there."

"You are always thinking of ways to make money, Joe," she laughed. "Look I have to go but call me later."

With that their conversation ended as abruptly as they always did. Still if it wasn't for the job Loren was in their relationship wouldn't have been able to last as long as it had. It was good that she was able to talk on the phone at work otherwise they would never get to chat especially as they were no longer able to talk online. So Joe picked up Reece, taking him back home via Cotteridge in search of the charity shops his mom had told him about in the week.

Joe walked Reece around Cotteridge. It was a beautiful summer's day and he hoped the fresh air would do them good, especially Reece who seemed to have his head stuck in front of the cursed games console more often than not. His real reason for being in Cotteridge was to check out the charity shops. There were four in total and Joe's mother had told him that he could get some great bargains which he could sell on the auction website Ebay. Joe had become quiet addicted to Ebay in the same way he had once been addicted to chat sites where he met numerous women. Of course now Joe only had eyes for one woman, Loren who he was deeply in love with.

The promise of cheap books or anything else for that matter proved completely fruitless. Joe's mother Rosetta had told him he could get at least four for a pound in one of the shops but after visiting all four he found this wasn't actually the case. What he did eventually find though was something he thought Reece would appreciate immensely. Joe pointed to a giant stuffed comical looking bull that was far bigger than Reece.

"Would you like that?" He asked his son pointing to the comically looking creature.

Reece eyes beamed with joy. He didn't answer with words simply nodding his head enthusiastically instead. He pointed at it with a hungry look in his child eyes. They said give me the big cow daddy. Give it to me now.

"If you want it you have to carry it yourself."

Reece didn't need telling twice he scooped up the giant stuffed Bull with both hands dragging the monstrously sized thing along the floor towards the counter.

Following behind Joe couldn't help but laugh to himself. The stuffed toy was absolutely huge dwarfing his five year old son in comparison. Paying for it at the counter it was worth the few pounds it cost to see how happy it made his son. After that they left Cotteridge by way of Taxi going straight back to Joe's parents. They wouldn't be in the caravan tonight. Summer or not it was too cold for Reece in the little bachelor pad of Joe's at night. After cooking them both a dinner of chicken nuggets, chips and baked beans they settled down for the evening. They watched Disney cartoons on DVD until Reece fell asleep with his belly full and his mind content.

With Reece settled Joe felt it was about time he called Loren perhaps not having heard from him she would be prepared to talk to him about things for a change.

"Hello, Joe. I didn't think you were going to call. Hope I haven't upset you." Loren sounded nervous when Joe called which was good he hated it when she got all arsy with him. He needed to make his point and was determined to do it.

"I'm fine I just think we need to sort things out instead of going around in circles,"

"Ok," Loren replied simply. There was a bit of hesitation in her voice.

"Look you know full well that the only way out is to accept my help. Take a loan from me a bank won't give you the money."

"I can't Joe. I have my pride you know."

"Do you have any other option?"

"Ok Joe I give in I will accept your help."

"Thank you."

"So does that make you happy?" she asked. Joe could tell she was tired from a long days shift from the weariness in her voice. She was doing her best to put on her usual cheery voice, but it just wasn't working.

"Yes a bit, but you really need to be making more of an effort. It's like people are always saying to me. It doesn't cost much to make a call. You can easily call me from a payphone. You don't seem to want to know me half the time."

"Look Joe I know what you're saying. Everything you're saying is right, and from now on I will be making more of an effort. I have said I will accept your help."

"So no more arguing then?" Joe said smiling to himself. It was the first time Loren had agreed with him. They had tried her way for months with nothing working. It was about time she give him a chance to help her out

"No definitely not I'm too tired to argue," laughed Loren. "So have you and Reece had a good day?"

"Yes. I bought him a giant stuffed cow. Reece named him Silly Moo."

"That's sweet. Well I'm all but finished Joe. I'm glad we have sorted things out. I promise to call you again as soon as I can."

The next morning Joe took Reece back to Isobel. It would be a week before he saw Reece again, two before he had him overnight, but Joe promised his son with a wry smile that Silly Moo, for that was the name they gave the large stuffed bull, would always be waiting for Reece at bedtimes when he stayed with his dad.

With Loren's thirty fifth Birthday approaching Joe wanted to do something very special. He had asked her one night when he was out at the cinema with some of his work friends via text what she would like. She jokingly responded that she wanted an expensive one carat diamond necklace with matching earrings. When he told her back in text that he could in no way do that for her as much as he would like to she said that a packet of Nik Nak crisps would suffice. I don't care much for presents she would often tell him as her Birthday drew near. Well I want to do something special he would tell her. So one night when he was supposed to be selling things on Ebay he started watching diamond earrings trying to find the perfect pair for Loren. It didn't take him long to find a pair. They were expensive, but as far as he was concerned they would be worth it to see the look of surprise on his soul mates face. He won them a few days later. He also bought her some fine luxury sets of underwear knowing full well that a gift such as that would only ever be seen by his eyes. He hoped they could spend a night together in a glitzy hotel. He would cover the bed in rose petals; take her for a romantic meal. It would all be such romantic wonderful surprise.

Joe was off work the following week. Loren had agreed not only to come see him one day, telling Adrian she had to work an extra day shift, but they would also spend a night out up town too. Things seemed to be really moving along since that Saturday night when she had accepted his help. At the beginning of the week Loren had promised to call Joe in the mornings after dropping the kids off at school. She stuck to her word calling him when she was able. It was a bit awkward with her finding out what day she could see him, but eventually they agreed on Wednesday daytime, as well as Thursday night. Joe had booked them tickets at Jongluers Comedy Club. It would be a great night. Joe spent most of his week working hard on Ebay in the day or going to town buying more things to sell at a profit online while talking to Loren when she was at work. She was on early shifts for most of the week which made it easy for them to talk, though Loren still seemed too busy. She told Joe that a staff member had left leaving everyone shorthanded but that it wouldn't affect her seeing him as she had promised. She really seemed to be making an effort which made Joe feel a bit more secure in their relationship than he had in a while. The one stumbling block was when she admitted she still couldn't accept Joe's money despite what she had said. After giving it some thought she told Joe she had decided she would fight to keep the house at all costs. Joe could understand it from her point of view but felt like he was again losing the battle to win her heart. Still he didn't want to ruin the plans they had made for that week so he kept quiet. In the evenings he didn't go out. Instead he stayed at home getting enough beers in to share between him and his father. He was having an ok week, but it would get better once Loren came into the picture.

He woke up early that Wednesday morning. It was going to be great seeing Loren in the daytime. To be able to make love with her with them both sober. He had bought a small bottle of wine, but that was more for her nerves than anything else. Despite the fact that as far as Joe was concerned she was the most attractive woman on earth she was very insecure about her body. Childbirth had given her a line of stretch marks along her tummy that she positively hated. It had been at the birth of her second Child, Her daughter Harriet who was fast approaching fourteen years of age. None of my other kids gave me stretch marks she always moaned to him on their nights together.

Joe didn't think anything of it he loved seeing her naked, to him she looked like a princess. He remembered telling her that to him it didn't matter. He gave a bad example by saying on the night they first made love that sand was smooth yet if you rain your fingers through it, then it too would have ripples. So as far as Joe was concerned that's all her stretch marks were. This he told her and was what he believed. Child birth was natural. Loren was a great mother. But all women have insecurities and that was hers. She would often ask if when they made love he could actually feel anything fearing that having four kids had mad her too loose down below. Joe could honestly say he had never enjoyed making love to any other woman so much.

So Joe was up early. He took a shower, made himself breakfast then went for a walk, something he had found himself doing often since his relationship with Loren had started nearly eight months ago. It was a lovely day the sun was shining, without a cloud in the sky. Joe had his usual anxieties of whether she would actually show even though she always did. All he could do was wait for her to call. She had told Adrian she was working a morning shift when in fact she had planned to spend the day watching movies while making love to Joe. So he walked feeling more and more wound up with panic until his phone rang and Loren told him she was on her way. She explained how she couldn't call earlier like she had planned; she was half an hour late in calling, as a neighbour had spotted her and given Loren a lift into work. This had put Loren on edge but she still had every intention of coming down and told him she was just ten minutes away in a taxi.

When Loren arrived everything was fine. Joe paid for her taxi as normal and they went to the caravan. Loren was far more nervous than normal. She mentioned the neighbour then how she saw a work colleague drive past as she waited outside the hospital for a taxi. Both of these had put her on edge. Also she knew full well she couldn't really drink all that much. Loren had always proved to be quite dominant especially when she had drunk a few to give her a bit of Dutch courage. Joe found he liked the fact that she was very shy with him this time. He told her without question to get into bed pouring her a small glass of wine for the sake of her nerves as she did so. He turned around while she undressed knowing how shy she was about her body. There would be no darkness that day. Once she was covered up with the bedclothes Joe put on the DVD they had both planned to watch. It was called

National Treasure, a Disney adventure moving starring Nicholas Cage one of their favourite actors. Joe had seen it when it was released in the cinema with his mates and at the time he had been on a break from Loren. Still he had texted her that night telling her how much he missed her and how the two main characters of Cage and his leading lady reminded him of the pair of them.

So they lay there together watching the movie wrapped in each other's nakedness, Joe hugging her from behind. It wasn't long before they started making love. Loren laughed as Joe took her from behind.

"What you laughing at," he smiled.

"You're fucking me as we watch a film. I'm trying to concentrate," she joked. "If I don't you will only tell me off."

At that they both laughed. They continued to make love with Loren pretending for as long as she could to watch national treasure. Her moans grew louder as Joe slowly thrust himself inside her. He had placed one of his hands firmly over her breasts squeezing her each time he thrust deep inside her. They soon forgot about the movie. Joe's DVD player wasn't exactly up too much it would occasionally stick or freeze the images on screen. This didn't bother either of them as they moved their hips in unison. They made love for over an hour before eventually they both orgasmed. Joe made sure Loren was fully pleasured by going down on her under the blankets. He loved doing that more than anything else. He had never been able to get over how good it felt. She was the only woman he had ever enjoyed oral sex with and he delighted in pleasing her that way. He didn't come up for air until he felt her legs her insides tighten, her legs wrap tightly around his body as she reached that crucial point. He came up for air and finished making love to her slowly until he too climaxed. As they finished watching the film Loren delighted in telling Joe how she had had one big orgasm as well as several little ones when he had disappeared under the blankets. Hearing the pleasure in her voice Joe could only go down again unable to stop repeating the act as he loved the sounds she made as he did his best to please her.

With the film over they chatted, and Joe talked about putting on another DVD before lying Loren back down ready to make love to her again.

"Stop," she told him suddenly clutching her head.

"What's the matter?" he asked her concerned that he may have done something wrong.

"It's nothing," she told him. "I just feel like I have a migraine coming on." She lay down on the bed turning her back to him. "I will be fine in a few moments just let me be for a while," she insisted.

So Joe lay there with her his mind full of concern and marvelling at how this was the first time any woman he had been with had ever cried not tonight I have a headache. Except this was Loren and she always loved their love making. They had made love so there was no need for this to be a lie. He knew from conversations he had with her in the past that she would sometimes have to take time off work with the excruciating pain she got from migraines.

"I'm going to have to go," she finally said sitting up slowly. "I have some special pills at home that will make me feel better."

"You can't!" protested Joe. "What about Adrian? Won't he be a bit suspicious when you're supposed to be working? Is it me have I done something to upset you?" He threw the questions at her in anger. He wasn't thinking. He just wanted the night to continue. He knew a part of him was being selfish, but he also knew Loren had a habit of making up reasons when she didn't want to reveal the truth.

"I knew you'd say that," she told him calmly.

"Well you know me. I don't know what to think. I thought we were having a good day. I can see you're in a great deal of pain. If you have to go I understand. I just want to know that we are okay."

"We are fine." She told him calmly. "We are still going to the comedy club tomorrow night. I've told Adrian I'm going out with work to the comedy club. Everything is fine. I just need to go home and lie down. He knows what I'm like when I get these. He will just take one look at me and know straight away."

"Okay." Joe conceded kissing her lightly. By now she had gotten dressed and was sitting at the edge of the bed. Getting dressed himself Joe ordered Loren a Taxi. They left the caravan and walked up the hill of his the cul-de-sac, holding hands as they went.

"I've really had a great morning Joe. I just need to get back and go straight to bed. Please don't call me once I'm in the taxi I know you will I know what you're like I just need peace and quiet."

"I understand." He told her. "I don't know I just never know where I stand with you. You know how I feel about you. I just sometimes think is it worth all the hassle."

"I do care about you, Joe. When you're not with me I really do think about you. I know it's probably easier for me as I have the kids keeping me busy and work but believe me I really care about you and know I don't show it enough."

It was at that moment that the taxi pulled up beside them. Joe hated letting her go. Always would. His time with Loren always seemed to be too short. It was only quarter to eleven. She was supposed to have spent several more hours with him. He wondered if the migraine was real or if she was just rushing off to take the morning after pill again even though she had insisted after the time at the hotel when she thought she might be pregnant that she would let fate decide.

He could do nothing though, but let her go yet again. Besides he would speak to her while she was at work tomorrow. He would be out with her tomorrow evening. He should have been happy. Something just didn't feel right. Joe felt very uneasy about the way things were going. They should have been getting better. They were seeing each other nearly once a week. Her husband had even found himself a girlfriend in Sheffield, and yet Joe was what still amounted to nothing more than Loren's dirty little secret. When they had first met she had told him she wanted to move out and get her place before Christmas. Loren's story soon changed to I will move out after Christmas as it won't be fair on the kids. Then they split up got back together and seemed to follow that cycle. She eventually said she would loan the money from him to rent a place and even that had changed even though initially she had seemed over the moon at the idea. Now she was adamant that she wanted to keep the house, with them both knowing full well that Adrian who didn't have a job would never budge unless she put her foot down. That was the trouble with Loren, all she ever wanted was a quiet life so she would never hassle her husband into leaving. God knows but after eighteen years of marriage he seemed to have her spellbound with some strange hold. The guy didn't work, did nothing around the house and yet she wouldn't get up the backbone to just chuck him out like any other sane woman in her circumstances would. Joe felt as though he was going nowhere in his relationship with Loren. If he was honest with himself he knew with things the way they were they would never go anywhere. They didn't have a future unless the woman could sort herself out. After eight months she seemed no closer to doing that.

So it was that Joe let her go. He did as she had asked and didn't bother calling her again that day, especially as he knew she would be unable to talk once she was back at home with her husband. He kept himself busy the rest of the day by going into town to get some packing materials for the things he was selling on Ebay. All the while thinking that the time he was spending in town should have been time spent making love with Loren. He ended up going into a computer game store to buy pre-owned console games that he could sell on at a profit. Even if they didn't manage to sell it was okay as Reece would get plenty of enjoyment out of them.

Having spent a good few hours in town Joe eventually returned home. He missed Loren. He always missed Loren. The idea of her being in the same house as her husband no matter how separated she told him they were just didn't work for him. He had an early night that evening. Loren would be in work on an early shift, finishing at three before getting ready at home to meet Joe in town for the comedy club.

That next day Loren didn't really get much chance to talk to Joe even though she texted him at every available opportunity. Seeing as their lovemaking had come to an abrupt end the previous day Joe was still highly aroused and spent the entire day texting Loren to let her know how much he missed her, how much he wanted her. She texted him telling him she didn't really have much credit left but would love to hear any fantasies he had that maybe they could turn into reality like that night at the hotel when they had explored each other until they could do no more. She thanked him for all his texts before she left giving him a quick call from a payphone in the hospital canteen, having run out of credit with all the texts she had sent him. One text really struck a chord with Joe. I think it's wonderful they way you put up with me, the text had read. She told him on the phone he could never be too horny for her; there would never be anything they could not do together. When the evening finally came, with Loren having left work Joe had started drinking already. In the past it would have been Loren who would turn up after having several drinks. Joe didn't want that this time. He wanted to be the crazy wild one this time. He intended to shock Loren that night if it was at all possible. He was tired of turning up with her already in the partying mood with him having to play catch up. In the past he would always watch what he drank with her so that he could look after her. Loren's a big girl she can look after herself.

So it was that they met in town. It was one of the few times Loren had been able to turn up wearing make-up and having done herself up for a night out. Adrian knew she was going to a comedy club. He didn't know she was still seeing Joe. It was raining lightly when they met so they headed into the same pub they always drank in while they waited for the rain to stop. It was actually a very hot day. The rain would soon vanish into nothing. They sat drinking lager as Joe explained he had already drunk a rather large bottle of wine. He ordered Loren several double vodka's with orange cordial. She preferred cordial with her Vodka rather than orange juice. It was her turn to play catch up. She sat there drinking with him, telling him how she was sick of how it was ok for Adrian to have his girlfriend in Sheffield while she was always under suspicion.

"I don't understand why you put up with him," Joe told her feeling angry. "The guy is so two faced. He was the one that told you that if you had a heart you wouldn't see anyone else while you were both living under the same bloody roof. Yet now that he has found someone it's ok for him to do it. God, Loren it's the whole reason I'm still a secret. I fucking hate it. Why don't you just do what any other woman would do and throw the guy out?"

"If only it were that simple Joe," she replied. "The house is in both our names. And I would like to think that when we do split that things go as well as possible for the sake of the kids."

"Yeah, but neither of you wants to move out. You both want the house. The situation will never change until you stand up to him. I really can't understand why he has such a hold on you. I'm just tired of being your dirty little secret."

"Well Adrian knows that from now on I will do what I want when I want. I've told him we may live in the same house but we live completely separate lives now. There's only so much I can take Joe. You know how I get I won't put up with him doing what he does in front of the kids for ever."

They eventually made their way to Jongluers, the comedy club halfway up Broad Street. Loren made sure they did their usual trick of stopping off at several bars on the way. It was as if the woman couldn't go a hundred yards without a drink in her hands Joe thought amused. Still he was the one that would be pissed that night he told himself laughing.

"What are you laughing at?"

"Nothing," Joe told Loren. "Just think we are in for another one of our mad crazy nights."

"Too right mate!"

So hand in hand as they always were when they went out together anywhere they made their way to the comedy club, checking in their jackets, before one of the clubs bar staff showed them to their seats. Chart music was playing as they entered making Loren dance all the way to the table.

Loren paid for the first set of drinks as they looked over the menu. They had arrived early so the place was pretty empty but Joe knew the place would soon fill up. The tickets he had got them were restricted view which meant their table was situated between a pillar. Still they could still see the stage perfectly from where they were. Joe had been there before on a Christmas night out with work two years before.

They decided to have a curry that was on the menu served with naan bread and chips. They were both starving so it didn't take them long to polish it off. Within fifteen minutes, their empty plates were taken away as the place began to fill up.

A young couple sat down at the table opposite them. The woman was thin with tattoos down both her arms, and short blonde curly hair. They introduced themselves as Sarah, and John. John was a slim guy who looked just a bit shorter than Joe with the same dark brown hair. As they chatted to the new arrivals at the table Joe ordered a pitcher of lager for him and Loren to share.

Loren ever in the mood for dancing pulled Joe up from his seat so they could dance before the comedy started. They were grinding against each other like animals on heat until the lights dimmed signalling the nights entertainment was about to start.

Sitting back down Loren noticed a short brown haired woman at a few tables away closer to the front stage. The woman had been casually looking around.

"What the fuck is she looking at? Has she never seen anyone have fun before? Stupid Cow. I'll have her. That bitch gives me the evils again and I'm going to shove this glass down her throat," she snarled. This strange ranting carried on for about ten minutes until Joe looked at her coldly. They were sitting at a table with another couple. Loren seemed to be deliberately causing a scene. Joe knew exactly what she was playing at. She was just mouthing off to get his attention. It was working.

"Look just stop it! Now!" His words were firm. Joe told her in no uncertain terms what he thought of her behaviour. He told her he knew she just wanted him to put her in her place and tell her off. He wasn't amused by her little game.

Smiling at him she moved from her seat to sit astride him, slowly moving her hips as she started to kiss him.

"You know what I thought the other night when I went to that Hen party," she told him softly as she continued to kiss him. "Everyone had gone home they had left me on my own. In the end I had to call Adrian. I thought to myself if Joe had been here he would have looked after me. I really missed you that night. It just wasn't the same without you. I always feel safe when you're with me as I know you take care of me."

"Thank you," Said Joe. It was good to know she had been thinking of him that night. She had called him when she was out. At first he had missed the call. She had been very drunk by the time she made it telling him that and saying she was having a great time dancing, but that she was thinking of him, that she did miss him.

The compere came on stage to do his first run of jokes before introducing the first act of the night. Joe took Loren's hand in his as their eyes turned to the stage.

They sat there laughing at the compere's joke it was turning out to be a wonderful evening. Every now and then Loren would move closer to Joe kissing him, her hands running over his chest. After a while Loren disappeared to the ladies. Joe just carried on watching as the first comedian of the night came on running through half his act leaving Joe in stitches. Still he found himself wondering what had happened to Loren. She always seemed to take ages in the bathroom, longer than any other woman he had met. He had an idea that she took those breaks to check up on her kids which he thought was perfectly understandable. Still she had been gone a long time. When the couple sitting opposite him starting asking questions Joe decided to go to the men's hopefully Loren would have returned by then. He just hoped she hadn't gotten into any trouble. She really had been gone a very long time, and Joe was getting worried.

Joe didn't reach the men's rest room. On passing the entrance to the ladies toilet's Loren grabbed him, dragging him inside. There was no one else in there except for a black woman in a blue overall, the toilet attendant. The look of alarm on her face when she saw Joe enter the room was priceless. It was as though she had just seen something from her nightmares creep into reality.

"It's ok he is my boyfriend," Loren told the toilet attendant as if that made his presence acceptable. She was laughing as she locked them both in a cubicle. She slammed him against the wall kissing him in a crazy frenzy. "Fuck me, fuck me," she kept repeating. Within seconds her jeans were down to her ankles and she demanded he enter her.

Joe had thought he was unshakable when it came to Loren that she had done everything she possibly could to surprise him. He was more turned on than he had ever been, and more than a little drunk. Moments later he was inside her taking her against the flimsy partition wall of the cubicle. It shook and rattled as though it would be ripped from the wall at any moment.

Loren whispered loudly in his ear for him to cum inside her as he thrust into her over and over again with rapid succession.

It wasn't going to happen. As exciting as it was he didn't feel comfortable with the toilet attendant shouting in the background that a man shouldn't be in there, threatening all the while to call security while not doing so. As much as she wanted to feel him explode inside her it just wasn't going to happen. It wasn't that he wasn't turned on it was just that with the old woman outside it was putting him off. In the end Loren pulled up her jeans telling him that they should go back to their seats.

"Thank you for the lovely surprise," he told her kissing her passionately as his hands firmly caressed her breasts.

"See Joe, you just never know with me do you," she laughed as they went back to their seats to the relief of the toilet attendant whose cheeks had never been more flush.

That wasn't the end of it though. Loren wanted more Joe found himself touching her intimately under the table as they tried to concentrate on the reason they had come to the club in the first place, the comedians. Joe ordered them another pitcher of lager which made him need the bathroom. He hadn't gone before, Loren had made him forget all about it. Loren followed him causing chaos in the men's which was packed. She jokingly locked herself in a cubicle alone. Joe eventually talked her out just before the attendant in the men's room called security.

By the time the second comedian was halfway through his act they were both so past sober it was ridiculous. They only had eyes for each other now and were paying hardly any attention to what was happening on the stage in front of them. One of the comedy club staff came over asking Joe to keep the noise down for the sake of the other staff.

Loren looked at Joe bemused. "What did he say?" she asked him.

"They think we are making too much noise."

"Ooooh can't be having that," she laughed. "Come on let's go find somewhere to dance." She stood up as if waiting for him to follow. "Come on Joe I want to boogie." She pulled at his arms trying to drag him from his seat. "Come on Joe you know I love you," she smiled.

"When the acts are all done we will be able to dance here it opens up into a big night club." Joe told her.

"Well I want to dance now," she laughed dragging him out of his chair down the stairs that led to the cloak room, where they collected their coats heading for Loren's Favourite club, Reflex.

She walked straight in without a problem. Joe on the other hand was barred entry, he was furious. The doorman a small Asian man wouldn't listen to reason. Joe tried to tell him that his girlfriend was in there. The Asian door man simply said that she would come out when she noticed he was gone. Fear filled Joe completely. Loren had had a lot to drink. When she was in that state she was oblivious to everything else around her. She would easily dance for over an hour before she noticed Joe was gone. A second door man a large bald headed white man came to the door. Joe convinced the man to find Loren for him. He gave the man her full name, and he got Loren out by getting her name called out over the DJ booth.

When she come out there was a look of thunder on her face. She obviously didn't like hearing her name being called out for all to hear over the loud speakers of the night club. Joe had been left with no choice. At first Loren argued with the door man, but by then they wouldn't let either of them in as before Joe had convinced the bald headed doorman to find Loren he had called the police on his mobile.

Outraged Loren stormed down Broad Street in a foul mood. The night wasn't going well at all.

"Why do you always have to go crazy Joe?" she shouted at him.

"I just did what I did to get you out. You were in there a good fifteen minutes didn't you notice I was gone?"

"I would have noticed eventually," she told him. Her mood had changed for the worse.

"Look let's not argue. I will get us into another club," he told her. Joe wasn't surprised that night's troubles had started at Reflex. It was the place they had tried to get into on their first night out together. In a way it was amusing to Joe that they had once again been barred entry, or at least he had. Still he couldn't shake the fact Loren had gone in without him. She hadn't looked back once. He kept hearing the bouncer's words in his head over and over again telling him that she would come out when she noticed he was gone. Maybe, maybe not, but perhaps she wasn't bothered perhaps she had done it on purpose. Loren had a self-destructive streak about her. When she drank it brought it out into the open.

So with all that on his mind he led Loren to another club. It wasn't to Loren's taste's as it was a rock club. He ordered them drinks only to find Loren sitting on a step refusing to dance. She actually appeared to be sulking. She hated the music. She wanted to leave. They barely stayed in there more than five minutes after Joe had paid the entrance fee as well as checked their coats in. They began arguing again, not that Joe could hear a word she was saying with the music blaring loudly all around him. He could read the expression on Loren's face well enough though to know she was in a foul mood with him. It wasn't exactly his fault he hadn't been able to get into the eighties club. Joe couldn't understand it. She was calling him a crazy person saying he was spoiling the night. She just wanted to dance. Joe could tell from the look on her face that a lot of her talk was down to how much she had drank. He had to do something to calm her down. As they left the rock club Joe remembered that there was another Reflex in town down Hurst Street in The Chinese quarter.

"We are going to Reflex," he told her.

"We can't we aren't allowed," she hissed walking alongside him with her hands folded.

"There's another one this way. We can get in there," he said with a smile. At that she took his hand in hers.

"That's right," he laughed hold onto me this time. Don't lose me in this one."

So holding hands they went to Birmingham's second Reflex. They just walked in not bothering to check in their jackets this time. Joe ordered them drinks even though they both probably had far too much already. It was getting late. Really Joe should have put her in a taxi and sent her home to her kids. It didn't cross his mind once. She was happy with him again now that she could dance. All Joe wanted was to see her smile. They danced the night away blissfully happy in each other's company. Joe even danced on the pole. Then as normal something happened to ruin what was supposed to have been a great night. A very fetching young man who looked a good few years older than Joe started dancing with Loren. She didn't seem to notice Joe staring. Joe was drunk, and getting very jealous. She chatted and danced with the guy for what Joe thought was too long, not to mention too close to be friendly. Eventually she came to his side to rest, explaining to Joe that the guy was gay. It was too late, and too many drinks for Joe to see reason. His mind was clouded with thoughts of her with this other man. Whether he was gay or not Joe didn't like it. They went to the bar to get more drinks. The good looking gay man was standing beside Loren as he ordered his own drinks. Joe decided he had to have a word. He went over to the guy to speak to him. All he wanted to do was say "look buddy this is my girlfriend can you leave off a bit." He knew Loren had a tendency to play up to other men in his presence just to see how far she could push him. Tonight he wasn't having it.

Joe never got the chance. What happened next was just too fast for him to comprehend. Strong arms pinned him from behind pulling him backwards. He was being thrown out. He had done nothing wrong. He had just wanted to talk to the guy. He watched as Loren walked off to the dance floor oblivious of what was happening to Joe. He didn't even think to call out to her he was too shocked to do anything other than go with the flow.

He found himself standing outside looking in at Loren as she carried on dancing with the guy who had invoked Joe's jealousy. After a while she sat down on a step inside the club. Joe was banging on the windows trying to her attention. She looked quite lonely sitting there. Joe wondered if she knew what had really happened to him.

It was freezing outside, not that Joe noticed. The alcohol in his system was keeping him warm as was the adrenaline pumped up by his anger at having been thrown out of the club for what he thought was no reason what so ever. He had no intention of starting a fight. He had only wanted to talk to the guy who had been dancing with his girlfriend. He had no idea what was going through her mind. Was she angry with him for what had happened in the other Reflex? If she knew what was going on then maybe she was punishing him? He didn't know all he knew was she was still in there without him. He managed to grab a young girl's attention. Pointing to Loren the girl told her someone was outside calling her. Wearing a bemused look on her face she walked outside. Once again the doormen closed the door refusing to let her back in.

"What's happening now?" she asked him a look of sheer puzzlement on her face.

"You tell me. One minute I was trying to talk to that bloke that was all over you the next they are grabbing me by my arms chucking me out."

"Yeah right Joe. I know you. You must have done something." She said in her best I'm not at all pleased with you ruining my night voice.

"I didn't honestly," Joe insisted.

"So now what?" she said her anger boiling over in a cloud of red mist in her eyes.

"Well I'm sure we can find another club," Joe said as they walked away from reflex. What he should have said was that it was late time for her to go home as they had both drank far too much. The thought never entered his mind.

They walked up the road in search of somewhere else to dance.

"I can't believe you didn't see what happened back there," He told her feeling frustrated. He was angry. He felt he had every right to be. Loren was taking it out on him just because she couldn't dance. Where was the concern for him, her boyfriend? He had gotten into trouble in both clubs. All night all he had done was try to make sure she had a good time. Nothing had worked. The night seemed to be spiralling out of control. The look on Loren's face showed she wasn't best pleased. All she could think about was dancing. They walked past some fencing that ran along a hotel. Joe spotted a darkened corner. Without thinking he pushed Loren towards the dark area. Hoping to calm her down with kisses. The fact was in the drunken state he was in he didn't know his own strength. He fell to the ground as he lost his footing. Loren tried to grab him, but fell over sprawling to the ground. She hit the concrete hard curling up into a ball.

The next thing Joe knew two men were standing over Loren as she huddled on the floor, crouching on her knees moaning that her back was in agony.

The two men consisted of a short bald guy in a brown suede jacket, and a tall dark haired guy in a tight t-shirt. They tried to help Loren up but she stayed on the floor.

"Are you okay?" he asked her not wanting to get to close with this strangers arriving the way they had. God knows how it must have looked to them as they had approached.

"Go away Joe. Leave me alone," Loren said softly from the floor. "It's over."

"Why? I haven't done anything. Come on stop being silly. Get up off the floor."

"I can't you have really hurt me." Her words grew in anger. The two men tried to calm them both down. "I really hate you Joe. You always go loopy. We are finished I never want to see you again."

"What?" exclaimed Joe the night becoming a blur he would never be able to quite remember. "We had a great night. This was an accident."

"Leave me alone," she screamed.

"You better do as the lady asks," interrupted the short bald man. "We will take care of her."

"No chance," replied Joe trying to keep calm.

Loren stood up screaming at him. She lashed out at him.

You want to hit me?" Joe shouted back pushing the short man away as his friend tried to hold back Loren. It was no use. Loren wanted to get at Joe. Joe wanted her to hit him. If that's what she wanted he told himself then let her do her worst. She did. She hit him several times in the head as hard as she could her fists balled up for maximum effect. She was swinging wildly. The woman had totally lost it.

"I hate you. You fucking bastard. I'll kill you." she screamed the words over and over again as she landed more blows on Joe. He took them all practically walking into them as the two men tried uselessly to pull them apart.

It was then that a police riot van pulled up alongside the road where they were fighting. The police rushed out splitting the enraged couple up.

Joe was glad they turned up when they did. The way things were going he would have let Loren put him in hospital. He tried to reason with one of the police officers telling him how Loren was actually married and that he had been seeing her for the last nine months. He said they didn't want any trouble and the night had just got out of hand. Loren wasn't being so calm. She was still screaming that she would kill Joe. The police officer that was talking to her warned her that if she didn't calm down that they would arrest her and that her husband would find out exactly what she had been up to. This seemed to shut her up for the time being. They made them go their separate ways then without charging them. All Joe could do was walk away with the two strangers that had intervened. It was the first time he had ever let Loren go home alone. The two strangers offered to take him for a game of pool. Joe was in no mood for games. He caught a taxi straight back home, trying to call Loren as he left

Birmingham city centre. The phone was engaged. She was more than likely calling Adrian to come pick her up. She wouldn't tell him what had happened. The night had started so well. Joe should have known sooner or later things would turn bad. As he lay in his caravan that night he only hoped he could salvage something the next morning.

Joe woke up early the next day. He had clean forgotten that he had to be at an intermediary meeting with Isobel at eleven o'clock. He was only reminded of it thanks to the automated calendar on his mobile beeping up a short message. Getting up he made his way into the house making some dry toast, and a cup of strong coffee. He had the worst kind of hang over imaginable. It was the sort that you knew full well you would suffer for the next twenty four hours no matter what you did. As the kettle boiled he drank two pints of water from a pint glass that lay just beside the kitchen sink, not thinking it would do much good. He tried calling Loren, but her mobile was switched off. He wasn't surprised she would have guessed that he would be ringing. She wouldn't dare turn the phone on while Adrian was around.

It was a few days later that he eventually heard from Loren again. He hadn't called her. In part it was because he just needed the space this time. The night had been a complete train wreck and he was becoming more than a bit depressed with the way things were heading between them. He just wished they could be happy. It just never seemed to go right, and yet when they were alone they were so passionate, so loving.

So one day he sat logged into chat, but not really paying much attention as he busied himself with online auctions. Then as he knew sooner or later would happen Loren popped up online when he least expected it. It was always the way. It wasn't that he had necessarily got used to it. It was just that certain patterns were forming. Adrian was away with his new girlfriend in Sheffield. Loren had been bound to pop online given the chance.

"Hello Joe," Loren typed turning her camera on so he knew it was her. "Look this is the last time we can chat like this. I need space. I have to get myself sorted." Reading what she put Joe found it hard to believe what she was saying.

"You always say that. One minute you want me the next you don't why can't we just talk on the phone at least like we used to? You still have the phone at work there is no need for you to keep doing this to me," he told her. He was pleading with her. He knew full well she would eventually change her mind. It was the waiting that hurt Joe the most. He was always worried for her. He found himself wondering how she was every day. He would never understand how she could carry on for three weeks at a time as if he meant nothing then come back to him as if he was the best thing in her life only for them to have one night of fun before it all ended again. Things should have been better not worse. He had put up with so much over the last nine months he hated the way she continually treated him.

"Well, why can't you just respect what I'm saying now? Just let me get on and sort myself out. You need to do the same. I am not saying I don't care or that we can never see each other again, but for now please just listen to what I'm saying."

"It's hard to listen to something I have heard over and over again."

"Well you will have to listen now as I won't be saying it again and I have made up my mind this time. It's over Joe. Look I have to go I'm sorry the kids want to use the pc."

At that Loren was gone leaving Joe with nothing but a black screen to look at. He was frustrated. He felt like crying, but knew tears wouldn't get her back. He couldn't believe how cold she had been.

It was the last straw for Joe to have Loren come online while Adrian was away in Sheffield insisting that it would be the last time they ever spoke. He asked her to call him but she wouldn't. He had been relentlessly texting her for days with no response. It was driving him absolutely insane. He knew full well that he was acting without any rationality what so ever. What else could he do it had all happened so many times before. He knew things would only get better then worse at some point then better again. After she logged off Joe went to the caravan. He still felt like crying as he did much of the time now. He believed himself to be a very strong man, certainly before he had met the woman he thought of as his soul mate, he had possessed a much greater strength. It was then that he decided he would not take any more of it. He would take the presents he had wrapped up in a parcel and deliver them to Loren personally. It wasn't for her he would do it but for his own peace of mind. The diamond earrings had been very expensive and the underwear not something he could give back as he just didn't have the heart. They were gifts meant for Loren and only her. Packing the box into a plastic bag he locked the caravan, sending her a text as he did: I don't care anymore. I have to do something for myself for a change, The text was deliberately ambiguous. He meant for it to be. Joe knew full well that if she realised what he was about to do that she would undoubtedly call him, easily talking him out of coming up to Sutton Coldfield while her husband was away to give Loren her birthday presents. He walked all the way to Cotteridge his mind racing, his heart pounding with fear. What was the worst she could do he asked himself, hit him again, or perhaps set her new dog, Bouncer, upon him, or maybe even call the police? He didn't care she was a very crazy woman but he had to do it. He loved her, wanted to prove to her how much. Joe hoped that it wouldn't end badly, that she would take his gifts at the door with grace. Getting To Cotteridge he caught the train into town. All the while he sent more vague texts to her to which he got only a few short responses with her telling him not to threaten her or that no one would tell her what to do. He simply texted back that he was doing something for himself for a change and that she knew full well that he had never, would never, threaten her or her children. He loved the woman completely he could no sooner harm a hair on her head than he could take his own life. He had proved that those three weeks before when he had pushed her to try and kiss her and calm her down. It had led to him goading her into attacking him. Punching him many times in the head, screaming at him that things were over and that she never wanted to see him again. She had told him she hated him that night. She had told him that on many other occasions. Her words no longer held any weight; especially words that would have cut him deep that were only fuelled by drink.

    The train arrived in Birmingham at New Street Station ten minutes later. Joe continued to send her the odd text. He got a response from her asking for him to come back online. He couldn't do that and could hardly text back with the reason why. He was halfway there already. All he needed to do next was get a bus to Sutton Coldfield.

    He waited by the bus stop shaking. This had to be the hardest thing Joe Hughes had ever attempted to do in his life. Loren had always insisted he should never under any circumstances come to her home. She had always said that things were between just the two of them. Only things weren't just between him and Loren. They never had been. Adrian was involved too. With the constant fighting Joe knew went on behind those closed does between the married couple they would always be a triangle rather than a couple. Then of course there were the children. As long as they both lived under the same roof their kids would always be affected. Reece was affected too. Joe had been unable to see him due to his emotional state after Loren had taken the knife to him. He wasn't seeing him that week end either due to his grandparents taking him on a short weekend break to Butlin's Holiday camp in Minehead. Whether he would be able to see his son again was debatable seeing as his own mother had let slip to Isobel what had gone on that terrible night. So now everyone was involved in one way or another. Joe wondered how a woman would have acted in his place had a woman been treated so badly by her married lover. Hell hath no fury like a woman scorned, the quote went, well maybe that was true to a point but maybe that's because it was unthinkable for anyone to believe such a thing could be reversed. No Joe would take the presents he had boxed up to the house. He had no intention of actually talking to Loren. He doubted she would talk to him. Maybe she would set her new dog on him, but talk to him no he didn't expect that. All Joe wanted to do was go up to the house ring the bell, leaving the presents on the doorstep, and leave. At least then he would have stuck true to himself.

It wasn't long until Joe found himself sitting staring into space on the bus to Sutton Coldfield. Now that he was on the bus there was no turning back. He had deliberately turned his mobile off for the time being so that there would be no chance of Loren talking him out of coming up to the house. He had left the house in a hurry, leaving with just his bus pass and only a couple of cigarettes. He only had two Royals left now and knew they wouldn't be enough to calm his nerves. With no way out he was on his way there was no turning back for Joe now. Sure in reality he could have just got off the bus at any time, catching a bus back to Birmingham city centre. He felt like he had no choice in the matter. Loren was done giving him the run around, this he hoped would be his final moment. If she did talk to him he would do his best to talk her into coming back to him despite the way she had hit him those weeks before. She was drunk, they both had been and he knew that foolishly he would always be able to forgive the woman almost anything.

He got off the bus in Sutton Town Centre. He knew where the house was from a map he had printed out off the internet. He turned his phone back on and immediately a text from Loren came through. Call me, it read. Joe would not. If she wanted to speak to him she would be calling him. It was too late now he was in Sutton it wouldn't take long for him to get to the house.

When she eventually did call her words were short, angry.

"Call me back. I don't have any credit on my mobile. I'm using my landline."

He had no choice. He had to talk to her to try and reason with her. She couldn't talk him into going back anyway now. He was already in Sutton Coldfield.

"Hello," he greeted her after dialling her number.

"Where are you?" she demanded

"I'm just taking a walk," He told her. It wasn't a lie. Joe really was taking a walk, except this time he wasn't walking around Kings Norton without a clue what to do, waiting for Loren to call, waiting for Loren to sort herself out.

"You had better not come to my house, Joe."

"I'm just walking. It's a free country. Need to clear my head. Look I don't know why you're doing this to me. You have admitted you care. You say you're going to miss me and that if we went out we would still have a good time.

What are you playing at?" It felt like he had told her this so many times before. He had though hadn't he? How many times had they been here before? He was sad the way things had turned out. Things should have been better. Now that Adrian had a girlfriend. Joe could not understand why Loren had ended things in such a self-destructive manner. She had always promised him she would give their relationship a proper chance when things with her and her husband were sorted. It seemed to Joe like she had taken a backward step.

"Look I know it's hard for you Joe. I just need time on my own. I'm not saying I will never speak to you again or that we can't possibly be friends but I just don't want anyone. I want to sort myself out and keep the house."

"Okay just do one thing for me then, and then I will give you your precious space. You always ask for it and always come back."

"Well what do you want from me, Joe?"

"Accept your presents. You know I won't take them back to the shop. I bought them for you and want you to have them. It would mean a lot to me."

"Okay and If I do that will you leave me alone?" Loren asked him.

"Yes," Joe told Loren.

"So when do you want to give them to me, Joe?"

"In about ten minutes," He told her unable to keep a wide grin from spreading across his face.

"Don't you dare come to the house, Joe," There was no longer any anger in her voice. Loren sounded tired. "Look I will meet you by the pub you always pass on the way to Hope Springs I will be there in ten minutes."

"That's fine with me," Joe replied. "See you shortly." He hung up.

It only took Joe another ten minutes to reach the pub she was talking about. It was called the Old Boot. He sat on a grass embankment a few metres away to wait for Loren to show up. As he waited he started to get paranoid wondering if she had called the police on him. That would be a laugh wouldn't it, he told himself, if the police arrested him for sitting out in the sun. Joe looked up and down the hill of rectory road expecting Loren to show up each time he saw someone new, it was never her. He rang her phone.

"Hiya," he said.

"I'm on my way," she told him. "I'll be five minutes I'm leaving now." Loren hung up. She didn't sound at all happy. Joe wasn't surprised. He knew deep down he was being stupid, if not more than a little impulsive. He just felt like he had to act.

Ten minutes later she arrived. She smiled at him with that same smile that had made him fall in love with her. She was wearing jeans and a small black sleeveless blouse. Joe thought she looked stunning.

"See I'm here Joe," she told him. "I can't stop long the kids are at home. It is good to see you."

Joe didn't know what to say he just handed the bag that held the box of presents to her.

"Thank you," she said taking the bag from him. "I just hope you took the earrings back."

"Don't be daft," he told her. "You know full well I wouldn't have done that. Despite anything you say today I love you. You do this time and time again. I am not giving up on what I believe to be the best thing that has ever happened to me he said." Joe was full of confidence. He was determined that she would listen to him no matter what it took.

"I won't change my mind," she told him.

"Well despite everything I still love you."

"You must be mad. How can you love me I'm crazy," she laughed."

Her mobile rang it was her eldest son wondering where she was,

"I've just popped to the shop to get some ice lollies. I bumped into a friend. I'm just chatting. I will be home shortly," she hung up. "See what it's like for me Joe I get no rest."

"Look I don't care whatever you say today," Joe told her firmly taking her hand in his. "Me and you are great together. We have loads in common."

"No I won't deny that Joe, whenever we go out we have a laugh, and we are very much alike. But still. My mind's made up. I still go out when I want. Me and Adrian live completely separate lives. I phoned him before I left to say I was coming to meet you. He wanted to know why, he thinks you're a psycho."

"Only because you told him I was," Joe interrupted.

"Well I just told him we have always got on, and that I wanted to end things on a nice note. I told him that it was none of his business at any rate. He said he knew I would be okay but that he disagreed with me seeing you again."

"You know he will bin your presents when you get back." Joe told her.

"No I will just tell him I didn't accept them. I'll put the somewhere safe. But thank you."

Joe hugged her then. "Don't worry I'm not going to kiss you." He was surprised that she returned his hug. "I do love you and I wont give up," Joe told her pulling away.

They chatted for another ten or fifteen minutes as Joe waited for a bus Loren told him would take him back into town. Joe just went over the same things time and again trying his best to convince her. At one point she even seemed to crack.

"If we started seeing each other you wouldn't be able to tell anyone. " she said before acting like she had been thinking out loud as she added "I just want to be on my own you have to respect that."

"Funny," laughed Joe," but you always say that every single time. Why can't you pick a new line, do things differently for once in your life?"

"I can't Joe."

"Why not would it really be so hard you know full well that if we went out next week we would have a great laugh? It would just be like old times. I will not throw away the best thing to happen in my life. I will never give up on you no matter what. Everything you have said to me I have heard before so don't expect me to listen. I will get you back even if I have to wait until you're a little old age pensioner." Joe kept his voice calm, as he fought for the women he loved. He didn't want her to see how much he was hurting. He wanted her to see the strong confident man she had fallen for so many months ago. That would be the only thing that would sway her to his side.

"I don't know," she told him. "Things aren't good for Adrian at home you know. I always have my back up with him. He hasn't got it easy."

"Maybe not," Joe told her, "but he gets to see you every day which is something I would give my life for."

"Well I have met you and accepted my presents gracefully so please just don't throw it back in my face, Joe."

"I wouldn't do that. I bought them for you. I just wanted you to see how much I cared for you. I feel better for seeing you."

"Yes it was good to see you without arguing," Loren replied smiling.

It was then that Joe's bus turned up. Loren pulled him close hugging him. "You take care,"

He sat on the bus, watching her wave him off. She was smiling. She had been happy to see him. It had been just like old times. He wished she had listened to reason. The spark was still there between them.

On returning home Joe logged onto his PC to check how he was doing on Ebay, automatically logging onto chat as he did so.

"Erm hello thought that was it?" Joe typed surprised to see that Loren had logged on.

"Thank you for the gifts. They're lovely, but you need to take the earrings back."

"I've been in the sun too long lol. You know when you spend too long in the sun you can tell lol I feel oven baked. And taking the earrings back is out of the question." Joe typed trying not to talk about the present as he moved the conversation on to the slight tan he had received on his walk through Sutton Coldfield

"Honestly."

"Look we left it well. I bought them for you." Joe couldn't believe what they were talking about.

"I think you've been done." Loren typed.

"The price tag online said 890 UDD which means they are worth 500 pounds. "I mean I did think they were a bit small but all I could afford."

that's not what I mean. I'm not trying to sound ungrateful at all."

"Did you like your other presents?" Joe asked her simply. He couldn't understand why she had logged on to complain. He wanted to move the conversation away from the earrings. She had to have liked some of the things he had bought her. The day had been really hard for him. It had been one of the hardest things he had ever done to go all the way to her home with the notion that she would only shout or scream at him, not that it had turned out that way.

"Yes. Thank you. They were all lovely. The earrings especially." Loren told him looking a bit flustered as she looked into the web camera.

"Ok. Look I'm just glad you like them was right about the La Senza stuff though right." Joe typed back.

"I must sound really awful."

"I know they are small but they are real diamonds and I said I wouldn't go on about it so you know just glad you liked what I got you, I know you won't wear anything not now anyway." Joe pleaded.

"I don't mean it like that."

"I'm sorry if you're a bit disappointed." Joe typed thinking he had let her down. Before that night when she had attacked him he had promised her the best birthday of her life. He told Loren the presents he got her would be the best in the world. He had exaggerated and even admitted that to her a few weeks before, but he thought she would have been pleased. She didn't sound pleased now. He didn't know why she seemed to be complaining.

"Don't be on the defensive."

"You know what I thought on the way back lol"

"what?" She typed.

"You were going to put the box in a bin on the way home lol."

"No I would never do that really they are lovely. Look I'm sorry for coming online hope I haven't upset you, I have to go do kids tea, bye Joe."

Bye." Typed Joe before adding, "Please have a think about what I said today. A proper think You know we are too good to just throw away.

"I will now go."

After logging off the PC Joe decided to send Loren another text. He had promised her he wouldn't text her anymore, but she had told him she wouldn't contact him and she had.

Sorry the earrings disappointed you his text said

It was only a few moments later that his phone rang. It was Loren again. Why couldn't she just leave him be?

"Look Joe the presents were lovely. I know how I must have just sounded online. But well you know I can be a bitch."

"That's true Ice," he laughed.

"It's just you said you had paid so much for them and well I just think you wasted your money."

"Do you like them?" He asked. It was the same question he had already asked online.

"Yes of course I do they're lovely. Everything you got me was great. I sound so ungrateful. I feel really bad. That's why I'm calling."

"That the only reason?"

"Okay no it's not the only reason. I've been thinking about what you said. Ever since you left you have been on my mind. I won't deny that. I don't know what to say."

"Look let's just give it another shot. Okay? I promise no more hassle from me. I will just see you when I can, when you can until you're sorted. Please."

"You know I went out Friday night. Could have had any bloke I wanted. But I told them all to piss off. I'm not like that. I just like to dance."

"That's ok."

"You jealous?" she asked.

"You can do whatever you like we aren't together anymore." Joe admitted. He knew she wanted him to have a problem with her going out. He didn't know why she was trying to make him jealous but he didn't let it get to him.

"Too right Mister. Told Adrian that. If he can swan of all the time to Sheffield I will do what I want when I want from now on."

"So what do you want from me?"

"I'd like to still see you yes."

"Thank you." He typed in response

"Look I have to go but I will pop on line later when the kids are in bed."

Later that evening Loren did as she had said she would. Things were never as over as she told him they would be. It was obvious she couldn't let go. Did she love him or was it just she didn't want anyone else to have him?!

"Hello Loren" Joe typed when she appeared on chat. He had been sitting on his PC browsing the internet waiting for her to turn up.

"2 minutes" Loren typed.

"OK." Joe waited then for Loren to reappear. When she did she invited him to accept her web camera as she always did with him doing the same. It was great seeing her again. He had a slim sense of hope in his heart that maybe they would be able to salvage something of their relationship after all.

"I can't understand why you said in the past that you felt proud to be out with me." Loren typed.

"It's because you're an amazing woman. You have a real sense of freedom about you. You're funny, domineering, crazy. I love everything about you and I just feel so good around you. Just wish that night we had stayed in the comedy club and not gone on anywhere else, with the air hitting us we both got even more pissed. If we hadn't left there things would have been fine." Joe responded.

"You can't change the past Joe. You just have to learn from your mistakes. Do you think you will ever find me boring?"

"No you're far too mad to ever be boring." He told her as he laughed.

I just think it would be good for us to go to a karaoke again like we did that first night. That's when I fell for you. You had a lovely voice. It was a good night."

"I will always remember the things you said to me that night you were so domineering I loved it when you said give me your tongue. I suppose I was scared of you from that night when you unexpectedly slapped me but I have never been shy with you. You always made me more open sexually."

"You were always the more experienced one Joe. And If it hadn't been for you we wouldn't have done half the things we did. I mean you know I would do anything with you. Sex should be fun, but well you certainly knew what you were doing."

"You have to be the craziest person I have ever known," typed Joe. "I never knew anyone who I felt so at ease with."

"Damn right boyyyyyyyyyyy."

"But it feels good to be able to relax completely with someone."

"Do u like the song by akon? lonely?"

"Yep."

"Mr lonely? I love it."

Loren sent him the song through chat and they listened to it together singing to each other even though they couldn't hear what the other was saying. They were having fun again. It was just like old times.

"Don't you have riveting chats with other women on here?"

"No." Joe shook his head.

"Think I'll start talking to all my old male friends on here."

"Nothing stopping you but you have my full attention you know that, and how I feel about you, and I can't do any more than I have done to make how I feel clear."

"Nope." She typed in response

"Today was hard for me," Joe confided. He stared into the screen trying to read her emotions. He wondered if he had really got through to Loren by going all the way to Sutton Coldfield and making his stand.

"It's obvious."

"Took guts you know that, as you're so domineering I knew if I answered the phone before I got to Sutton thought you would talk me out of it and tell me off, do u understand what a grand gesture I tried to make?"

"lol but you were lucky I was in a good mood."

"I didn't expect you to be but I had to try one last time to let you know how I feel. I thought you would set the dog on me lol. I'm glad you didn't."

"So are how do you feel now Joe?"

"I'm happier. I promise I won't be bothering you anymore this time."

"Good."

"So how do you feel?"

"Better," laughed Loren, "Hey that's good for me," she joked. They both know it was hard for Loren to open up about how she truly felt. Joe just hoped that in time she would be able to express her feelings more when Adrian was finally out of the picture.

"Well it's late I had better go," Joe told her, "Will you be on tomorrow?"

"When the kids are in bed then yes." She typed back.

At that their chatting for the night was over. The following night they would be able to talk again. Hopefully Loren would stay on long enough for Joe to be able to wish her a happy Birthday.

So that following evening Joe logged onto his pc at quarter to ten. Loren was there waiting for him. He accepted her invitation for her web camera offering. As had happened time and time again they both looked into each other eyes over cyberspace.

"Where have you been?" she typed. "I was just about to start chatting to all my old male friends."

"I knew you wouldn't be on early. I wanted to make sure the kids were all in bed before I came online."

"When did u know u loved me?"

"I liked you the moment I met u but I fell for you that night when I saw what you were really like, and when I felt so proud to be out with u and to look out for you and then I told you and you couldn't believe it, and I woke up the next day and thought wow everything I said was true how can it happen just like that? But It did."

"Our first night out when we sang karaoke?" she asked.

"Yes. I remember buying the stuff in La Senza and thinking she will look stunning." Joe typed changing the subject from the past.

"Notttttttttttttttt," came Loren's reply."

"Did u bother to try any of it on?"

"Not yet I'll show you hold on. 1 min." Loren disappeared from view.

Joe couldn't believe his luck. She was going to try on the presents he had bought her. He had hoped in some vague sense that this would happen, but never truly believed it. It was just wishful thinking.

"You look amazing, I had planned to remove them personally.... never going to happen now." He told her as she came in wearing the bra of the first set of lingerie he had bought her. It was a two piece set, thong with bra. The bar was pink with a floral green design. Loren had previously told him in a text that her favourite colours were green and brown. Her pyjama's she wore on cam a lot were pink. Joe had found that set combined everything that Loren liked. She looked amazing

"That's the first one." She left the view of the web camera again, obviously trying on the other piece he had bought her.

"You looked stunning by the way I know I got the right ones." He typed the words even though she wasn't there. He knew she would be able to read them on her return.

"Wow now that's even better I could have made love to u all night in that." He typed thinking that if he was there with her then that that was exactly what they would end up doing.."

"Piss off," she typed laughing.

"Move it down or stand up so I can see it. I've suddenly gone all funny, what a cleavage."

"Which do you like the best?" she asked

"That one, the one you're wearing now."

"Why?"

"I imagined you astride me in that when I bought it. That was the intent as I know how you feel. I knew with that being a one piece it would cover your stomach and you would feel more comfy covered and let yourself go. It's the first thing I bought when I went into the shop, just saw it and thought I have to see you wearing that and make love to you in that. "Do you like it then?"

"Yes. Don't know when I'd wear it. lol not your everyday underwear." She typed.

"For special occasions lol with someone nice like maybe your birthday."

"Wish I could, but like I told you I'm taking the kids to the Wacky Warehouse with Adrian when he gets back from his girlfriends."

"It doesn't matter least we are back to what we can class as normal." He conceded.

"You know what time I was born?" Loren type moving the subject away from sex.

"No."

"1.10 on a Sunday morning. I was two months early."

"So you were supposed to have been born on the same day as me." Joe typed. He wasn't surprised at all. After all they had said they were soul mates.

"Yep but six years earlier."

"So what time are you all off to the wacky warehouse tomorrow and do you ever jump in the balls?"

"I used to play in there but it kills your feet." Loren laughed at this waving her feet in front of the camera as if to emphasis her point.

"You make me happier than anyone when I'm with you." Joe typed.

"Why?"

"I feel at peace like I am with a kindred spirit. I can just be me. I just hope I can always make you happy."

"I'm listening to Baby Love." She told him and sent him the track to listen to as she did.

"Just asking but I take it you won't be able to phone tomorrow? Guess that's why you're here now so I can wish you a happy birthday"

"Yes. Adrian's going to be back from Donna's tomorrow so probably won't be able to call, but I thought it would be nice if you could be the first one to wish me a happy birthday."

"Just like Christmas," Joe typed, "we saw that in together too. I remember "I couldn't sleep and had a hunch you would be on and you were."

"I won't be online tomorrow." Loren told him. She was dancing away to whatever music she was currently playing. Her head bobbed from side to side.

"It's ok I understand and I won't hassle you anymore, just get yourself sorted and see me when you can."

"I look roughhhhhhh." Loren typed. She pulled a mock sad face on camera for Joe.

"You look fine." Joe insisted. He laughed at her pretend sadness.

"Don't tell me that I have eyes can look in the mirror Joe."

"And you know what my eyes tell me. With Loren I'm like martini. Anytime any place anywhere."

"I think you would be inside me twenty four seven if you could," Loren typed back laughing.

"That's true," Joe told her smiling back at her. It was gone twelve now. "Happy Birthday Loren. I hope you have a fantastic day tomorrow and I really am glad you liked all of your presents."

She nodded happily from her side of cyberspace. She was still wearing the piece of lingerie he liked the most. He was happy again. For how long it would last he didn't know. Joe had learned the hard way that putting Loren under any kind of pressure just wouldn't work. If she was ever to leave Adrian or have him leave her she needed to do it on her own without anyone pushing her into it.

"Maybe one day you can wear those things with me on a special occasions," he typed a devilish grin spreading over his face.

"Too right mate," Loren typed back. "Well I had better let you get to bed you have work in the morning, and as it's my birthday I will be cleaning the house."

So they bid each other good night. Joe went back to his caravan feeling calmer than he had done in several weeks, glad to have sorted things out with Loren for what he knew was likely only the time being. He knew if they did go out again in the near future he would have to watch his drinking. It hadn't done them any good lately to have them both getting completely off their faces.

Settling down for a quite night in his caravan Joe couldn't help but think of Loren. His trip to Sutton Coldfield to see her had paid off. At last they seemed to be back on track, again. He had promised her that he would hassle her no more, let her sort herself out; if she actually could. Those last two nights online had been wonderful. The time they spent till the early hours chatting like old times while she sent him some of their favourite songs had been wonderful. She had loved the presents he had taken to her he knew that. So now with the day of her birthday upon him he had gone to work happy knowing he had stayed up that previous night long enough to be the first person to wish her a happy birthday. With a book in hand entitled The Dark Tower, Supposedly Stephen Kings last work of fiction if the rumours about the great authors retirement were to be believed, Joe settled down and began to read. For an hour he read through the book. Occasionally he would stop to light up a cigarette. He smoked Royals now always would they were what Loren smoked. They also proved slightly cheaper than the brand he used to smoke. After an hour of reading, with his mind always drifting to Loren and the fact that she was out somewhere enjoying a meal with her family, providing her husband had indeed returned from his girlfriends in Sheffield that was, Joe's phone rang. He didn't recognise the number but instantly recognised the voice.

"I'm coming to see you," It was Loren. Who else would it be?

"Where are you?" Joe asked. This was a bolt out of the blue. He never thought he would be seeing her on her Birthday of all days. He had resigned himself to a quiet night in. That would be the last thing he would be getting now.

"I'm in a taxi. The driver is letting me use his phone as I don't have any credit. What do you want me to do? Do you want to meet me in town or come to you?"

"You come here," Joe told her without hesitation. After there last night up town had ended in her assaulting him he wanted nothing more than to have a relatively quiet night in, besides if he could get her to the safety of the caravan nothing could go wrong there. They could dance in the caravan despite it being cramped. He would let her play all her favourite songs. There was no chance he would be going to town with her that night no chance at all. He could understand she wanted to go to town. It was her big day and all the woman wanted to do was dance. Joe just couldn't risk them having another argument.

"Okay," she replied

"Look I will call you back in ten minutes or so I take it your quite a distance away at the moment?"

"Yes."

"

"Good I need to get some money from a cash machine. Then I can go get us some wine for the evening."

"Can you get a bottle of Pernod too? My mom used to love that. I've been thinking about her a lot today. Please Joe it's my birthday."

"You know I will get you whatever you want. I have never let you down," He told her.

"Thank you, Joe. Just had a really bad time with Adrian, again. He kept calling me a fish I only had two drinks. He wouldn't even talk to me. He spent the entire time texting his girlfriend and it was me that had to give him the money to get credit."

"Do you even have money to pay for your taxi?" He asked her cutting her short. They didn't have time to talk with her on her way. They would have plenty of time later.

"No," she replied. "Told the kids I'm going out dancing. Adrian just looked at me and said he saw it coming."

Joe wasn't surprised. It was always the way. He knew it was a drain on him. He was supposed to be saving up to rent his own place. Every time his money would rise Loren would come back to him they would have a few mad nights out and he would be a few hundred pounds worse off. Sure with the help of all the things he sold on Ebay he soon got the money back, but that wasn't the point. Things just couldn't keep going on the way they were. They always seemed to be running around in circles like headless chickens without a clue to what they really were doing. Joe knew exactly what he wanted. He wanted to have a normal relationship with Loren without any of this constant hassle. The trouble was Loren never seemed to know what she wanted from life. It was obvious she cared for him, but since that first time they made love her feelings had grown cold, she had raised her guard and rarely if ever told him those words of I love you. It wasn't the first time she had called him out of the blue expecting him to drop everything to come to her aid. He couldn't help himself. Letting Loren down was never something Joe would never be capable of. Still he planned not to drink that night. Well he would probably have one birthday drink with her but after that no more. It was the best news he could have had. He was getting to spend time with the woman he loved on her birthday.

"I'll call you back," he replied before hanging up.

Time was very short he knew that. It wouldn't take Loren longer than thirty minutes or so to get to him. He quickly tidied the caravan, making the bed, throwing any rubbish into a black bin liner he kept in the corner, and spraying some strawberry scented air freshener around until the fragrance almost chocked him. Grabbing his jacket he made his way as quickly as he could to the local off licence, buying a few bottles of wine after getting some money out of the cash machine that sat in the shops corner.

As he headed back to the caravan Joe called up Loren.

"Where are you now?" he asked her when she picked up.

"I'm just turning into the top of your grove," she replied. "I almost thought you had decided not to call me back."

"Whenever have I let you down?" he asked her sprinting past the caravan to the top of the hill to find Loren's taxi before him.

"Never," she replied looking at him with a smile that told him she had probably had a bit too much to drink already.

"The lady says you're paying. She's certainly an expensive one." Piped the elderly taxi driver.

"She's a real handful," was all Joe could muster as he paid the man.

He quickly led Loren back to the place they had made love so many times before. He didn't want his parents to catch sight of her. His mom knew exactly who had assaulted him, and while his father didn't know he figured he would still recognise her. The last thing he wanted on Loren's Birthday was any kind of argument with anyone. He just wanted to try and make it as good a night as possible

"I wanted to go dancing." She told him as he closed the door.

"you can dance here," he told here firmly. "after what happened last time me and you went to town I think that's the last thing we need, beside it will be good for us to spend some quality if not quiet time together"

So he poured them some Pernod into two pint glasses mixed with blackcurrant cordial and lemonade and sat back in the bed as he watched her dance.

"I want no talk of relationships tonight", she told him.

"What do you mean by that?" he asked confused. She had after all come to see him what was she playing at.

"You know what I mean!"

"I don't you scare me."

"Why you getting funny with me Joe," she hissed. "That day you came to see me to give me my presents you were so confident it was a real turn on now you're acting all scared. It's not helping matters.

Joe closed his eyes and thought it over. Fuck it he thought she wants me to be Mr Cool I'll give it to her for one more night. Opening his eyes he took her in his arms and pushed her against the caravan cupboard. She tried to move but he held her fast kissing her passionately. His hands moved quickly beneath her top squeezing her breasts.

"That's more like the Joe I want, "Loren grinned as she batted her eyelids at him as if to say I'm just little old me, pretty sweet innocent Loren. Joe knew differently. She was a woman that knew full well how to use her sexuality to get whatever she wanted from anyone. She gave him the look she always did when she was horny. She always played hard to get but wanted Joe to be forceful. She loved it when he just took her.

He threw her down onto the bed. She wanted him to be masterful in charge for all of her so called domineering ways she loved it when Joe just took her. With her spread out on his bed he pulled down her jeans. He didn't stop to undress her completely he simply pulled down his own jeans to his knees and slid himself inside her.

"What do you think you're doing," she grinned.

"Don't say anything." Joe told her lifting off her top and covering her breasts with his hungry lips.

They made love as they always did. It was fun, energetic, exciting, passionate, everything it should be. Loren would wander off naked to change the song every so often before Joe dragged her back to the bed to make love to her some more. When she fought him as she always playfully did he made love to her wherever he could. When she knelt down beside the Hi-Fi to change the CD Joe made sure to take advantage of her being on all fours and naked. They had the wildest sex life two people could ever have. Still Joe wanted more than that and knew full well that in the morning he would feel sad with her gone. Loren would feel guilt of course. She always felt depressed the day after drinking, or maybe it was the day after seeing Joe. He didn't really like thinking too hard on what it really was.

As normal as Loren would sit up, tell Joe about her insecurities, how her stretch marks made her feel, how the fact she had bared four wonderful children made her feel like Joe wouldn't be able to feel anything when he was inside her. As always Joe told her the truth. He had never enjoyed lovemaking with anyone as much as he did with Loren. It was only with Loren that he seemed to see it as more than just sex. It was like a meeting of two souls. He couldn't explain it any other way other than to say maybe the only real reason it was different with Loren was that he was in love with her.

Loren had full control of the music that night. It was her birthday after all, as far as Joe was concerned the woman could do no wrong. It was her special night and she could do whatever the hell she liked. He only wished he had been able to make love to her in the presents he had bought her; he would have done anything to see her wearing those earrings, that underwear. Still he had seen her give him a little fashion show the night before on the web camera, and she had looked stunning.

It must have been around half past two when Joe still making love to Loren grabbed his phone off the television meaning to check the time. After that night he could never remember if he actually got the chance. Loren pushed him away. She started screaming at him.

"What the fuck are you doing? How dare you?"

Joe didn't have a clue what she was going on about. All he could do was watch as she stood up and got up from the bed.

"Give me your phone!" Loren demanded making a grab for it.

"What the hell is wrong? Calm down," he told her hiding his phone behind his back out of her reach.

"That's it I'm going," she screamed her voice rising. Joe wondered if the neighbours could hear the commotion. If things escalated any further then they soon would hear if they couldn't already not to mention Joe's parents.

"Ok, you win," Joe told her in an angry whisper, "Take the dammed thing."

Snatching his phone from him she knelt on the bed running through his address book at all the numbers. Joe had no idea what she was doing. She hadn't told him what she expected to find on his phone. All he knew was she was acting crazy again. He had thought being in the caravan would be a safe bet that nothing could go wrong. Loren was proving him wrong. It was like she always said about herself, you never know what's going to happen with me Joe.

Joe was pissed. Far too many glasses of wine had been the cause of that. He wasn't going to let her call anyone on his phone if that was her intent. He snatched the phone back from her and tipped her handbag over looking for her phone instead. Afterwards he would realise how crazy his actions were.

"Why don't you let me look at your bloody phone" He screamed back at her his face full of anger.

"You're a fucking Nutter, Joe you always do this go fucking loopy. I'm fucking going." The look on her face then was the same look he had seen before it was the same way she used to look at Adrian as he talked to her off screen when they used to chat online. It was a look that said she hated him. She had flipped again.

Where was she going to go, she was stark naked and it was the early hours of the morning. Joe didn't need this crap, he had to be up at seven for an early start at work. He grabbed her holding her down on the bed. "Look just calm down your arguing over bloody nothing." He told her hoping that some amount of reason was in his voice as he spoke to her.

"Let me go, Joe," she said spitting her words into his face.

He was only making things worse. She had lost it like she had that night when she had assaulted him, the same way she had lost in the night of the concert. There was nothing he could do when she was in this frame of mind. Still what was he supposed to do let her run out naked?! He needed to calm her down.

It was then that he spotted the knife Loren held in her hand, glistening in the darkness of the caravan. In all the commotion he hadn't noticed her take it out of her bag. "Let me go Joe, she told him calmly," Or I'll fucking stab you I swear to god."

Joe ignored her as she swiped the knife at his chest cutting him. He couldn't feel a thing he was too angry, maybe too intoxicated with wine. He pulled her hands away from his chest, closing his hand around hers.

"Go on then stab me if that's how little you care," he told her calmly wondering how psychotic they both would have seemed to anyone walking by. He held his hand around hers as the knife edge pricked his abdomen. The knife went in slightly who was pushing didn't matter the fact was neither of them would let go. Then with his fear finally overcoming him Joe rolled over to his side. He watched as she raced out of the caravan slashing his back as she went. Luckily it had been purely by accident she had just waved the knife at him as she had ran out, wearing nothing but her crazy stare. Still he could feel the warmth of his own blood. She had done more than scratch him with the blade. So she was stark naked about to do something that would only end badly. The last time she had run off she had roamed the streets. At least on the night of the concert she had put her clothes back on first. Joe wondered how much more crazy she could possibly get. Could the night possibly get any worse? It was supposed to be a special evening with them both celebrating her birthday together. They had been making love only moments before, he had even sung to her with a loving look in his eyes as he had done so. All that was ruined now, she had done it again, gone ballistic. He had no way to restrain her it was just making her even worse.

Hearing her bang on his parent's door repeatedly screaming he raced out after her. Things were going from bad to impossibly worse. Joe realised he had no way of controlling the situation. Why hadn't he learnt his lesson the night they had gotten to the comedy club? How stupid could he have been?

From that point on the night became nothing more than a chaotic blur. Joe remembered the look of horror on his father's face as he saw Loren standing naked before him. He had ushered them both quickly inside poking his head out the door wondering how many of the neighbours had been awoken by the trouble his son had brought to his door step. Joe had tried to reason with his father. Tried to tell him it wasn't how it looked. So how was it really? They both were naked, pissed out of their heads screaming like a pair of mad people. So how on earth could Joe Hughes expect his father to listen to him the state he must have looked? Joe's Father simply pushed Loren into the kitchen calling her a slag. By then the damage had already been done. Moments before she had sat upon the living room sofa with just a pillow to cover her blushes as she dialled the police. Loren told them to come quickly giving out an address Joe was surprised to find she knew exactly including the postcode. Joe found the whole thing mind blowing. Loren had gone completely, she had flipped, brought his parents into the whole mess, and yet she sat there calling the police. Eventually they both got dressed as the arguing continued. Joe was still trying to explain things to his dad telling him to treat him like an adult. His father flipped out at that point punching Joe in the head continually.

"Why are you fighting your dad?" screamed Loren from the kitchen doorway. She was still naked except for the pillow she held to her stomach.

Joe couldn't believe what was happening. He looked at Loren. How vain she was to be thinking of her body, her stomach, when he was being attacked by his own father in the place he called home. If she was that bothered why didn't the woman get dressed before causing such a big scene?

If it wasn't for Joe's younger brother Gary leaping down the stairs to intervene, then who knows what would have happened. Joe's father would have likely killed him, Joe just stood there not feeling the punches too distraught over what was happening. Or his father with his weak heart would have collapsed of a heart attack.

Loren stood half clothed apologizing to Joe's mother who looked down upon her with hateful eyes. Yet for Joe there was no compassion in her eyes, no regret at what she had done. Loren looked completely emotionless. She blamed Joe for everything.

There was a knock at the door.

"It's the police," Joe told everyone. The arguing suddenly seized then with the law at the door everyone stopped shouting as they realized how far the situation had gone. An eerie calm descended upon Joe's family home that night, and he feared things would never be the same again.

Joe's father was clutching his chest. He may have hit his son in a moment of anger, something he would confide in his son days later that he regretted immensely, but the man had a very weak heart. If the police had not arrived when they did he would have more than likely had a repeat of the heart attack he had had a little over twelve months before.

"It's me you want" Joe told a youngish looking police officer with dark hair standing a good four inches above Joe. He was tired, confused, he didn't know what they hell was happening.

They cuffed him without question bustling him off to an awaiting squad car. They fetched him his jumper from the caravan. Joe didn't realise until he got to the station, spending the night in the cells despite his protests that he had done nothing wrong, that Loren too had been arrested. It wasn't until the following morning as he spoke to his mother that he found out what had gone on after he had been led away.

The police, a male and female officer had questioned Loren.

"Why did you stab him?" They had asked her. "Did he hit you or hurt you in any way?"

"No," she had told them. His mother had told him the look on her face was as though she didn't care about anything or anyone. Joe believed that the look on Loren's face at that time was probably more one of puzzlement of a woman completely smashed out of her face on booze. He didn't say this to his mother. Rosetta had seen for herself on the night how pissed the pair of them had been. So for that matter had his neighbours. Joe asked him his mother to tell him more of what had happened after he had been led away in his handcuffs. Rosetta did her best to fill her son in on all the gory details.

"So why did you do it?" the policewoman had asked Loren obviously trying to get to the bottom of things.

"He held me down."

"And that gives you reason to stab him?" the police woman had asked puzzled.

"No," was all Loren could say.

Joe wished he could have been a fly on the wall at that moment. He wished he hadn't gone to the door with his arms outstretched to be handcuffed. Still he had been drunk. At the time it had been the most logical thing to do in the world. Given hindsight he should have invited the police into the house letting the whole situation defuse. Perhaps if he hadn't have just told them to take him away then maybe there would have been no arrests that night. Then Adrian would never know.

The absurd thing was they even let her keep hold of her knife for a time. Until Joe's father questioned them on it, only then did they confiscate what Joe's father had labelled a dangerous weapon.

So they had both been arrested that night. The medical doctor on hand at the station made a complete note of Joe's injuries before he was led back to his cell where he slept after tossing and turning for what couldn't have been very long. It had been a long night. The police gave him water and cigarettes when he asked, but ignored his pleas of innocence as he shouted through the door that he shouldn't be there.

He was released the following morning just after seven o'clock without charge. The police told him they would call him later. He was puzzled didn't understand, would Loren be pressing charges of some kind? No they had told him that's not why they would be calling. They wanted to give him time to think. They wanted him to press charges against her.

He was taken home by his father on a very silent drive. He couldn't get his head around that previous night.

He was still heavily pissed on wine and Pernod. In time he would calm down. But at that moment and for the rest of the day he resented his father for his actions. His father could have easily killed him that night, finishing what Loren had started.

   As far as work went Joe phoned up his friend Larry who was the deputy to their team leader Sally. He explained everything to Larry asking him to have a private word with Sally before he called in himself. After speaking to Larry he called the doctors. He needed some time off, needed to sort his head out big time. The last nine months of his life had been one big rollercoaster through hell with only a few bright moments. Every time he had enjoyed Loren's company the day after always spelt disaster. He decided that he would need a long rest from work, perhaps even counselling so that he could perhaps understand why he kept taking her back after everything she did to him. Even then as he booked his appointment he wanted to be with her. Despite her pulling the knife on him Joe still loved her same as he ever did. The previous night had been a complete shock to him, yet a nagging part of his mind told him he should have seen it coming, especially after she had assaulted him several weeks before.

   Joe spent most of the rest of that day in bed sleeping off the alcohol still in his system.. He didn't want to think of how badly things had turned out with him, and
Loren. They were supposed to have been soul mates. He couldn't sleep he just tossed, and turned. Eventually he got up going down stairs to make himself a coffee. Logging onto his PC he found he had a rather nasty email from Adrian waiting for him on Chatsmart.

Well I just had a nice call from Kings Heath Police Station. Soooo funny ha-ha. Anyway you are seriously disturbed. I really don't know what she saw in you. You are mental but you don't realise that do you. You've got emotional problems. Seriously you've got to sort yourself out. The two of you together won't do either of you any good. Hey if she liked you it wouldn't bother me but I know she doesn't but for some reason you keep pestering her and she keeps giving in. Why I don't know. Did you know on Friday night she went out with another bloke she met off the net called Rueben? I bet she didn't tell you that did she? She's not the person you think she is. If you want a quiet and happy life find someone else! And for what it's worth I Mean that sincerely. Anyway have fun in the police station and I hope your wounds aren't too painful ha-ha

Joe didn't know what to think. Loren had told him she had gone out the Friday before she had seen him. She had told him that she had been out with friends from work dancing the night away in Reflex up town. Joe didn't know what to believe about this man Adrian suggested she had been seeing behind his back. All he knew was that the woman he loved had assaulted him, stabbed him, and continually lied to him. It was the last straw. Joe always thought he was a very strong person. He just couldn't take any more of the games. He sat there at the stool on his PC and wept. He let the tears flow wanted them all out, he just wanted to be able to let go. When he had cried until he could cry no more the loss was still there. He was in pain. He had to have answers. He decided he would call Loren on her mobile, that was if she hadn't changed the number again like she had after the Darren Hayes night out. Joe had to find out the truth about this man Adrian had called Rueben. Regardless of whether he was just a friend or not Joe had to know what had really happened that night. Loren had kept it hidden from him which told Joe only one thing. Her and this other man had to be more than friends or why else would she have kept it a secret. Okay so they technically hadn't been together then, but they had always had bust ups in the past. Joe had always stayed faithful. It made him wonder how many other things Loren had hidden from him in the past ten months.

   Setting up a fake profile as Loren on Chatsmart, Joe spent several nights finding out all he could about the people she talked to hoping to find out who Rueben was. It didn't work. All it did was open up more trouble. He found out she had met someone else in the past just before she had met him. Joe managed to get the guys mobile number, Joe never asked him his name, but found that he had met Loren shortly before Joe had. So the fact that Loren had told him she had never met anyone off the internet had been a lie. He spoke to another guy called James who had been a friend to Loren for the last two years. James insisted that they were just friends. He knew nothing about Joe. It was as Joe had always feared he was nothing but a bit on the side. Eventually Joe gave up looking for Rueben. Instead he did what he had in the past. He concentrated on Adrian. One evening he managed to hack into the chat account that belonged to Loren's husband. Joe was really losing his grip on his sanity by that point. He found the email address that belonged to Donna. He took it upon himself then to do as much damage to Adrian's relationship with the woman as he possibly could. He told Donna in several emails how Adrian was a gambler, how he would on occasion hit his wife, not to mention the time he had forced her into sex. This caused chaos. It didn't make Joe feel any better. All he wanted was to hurt Adrian the way he had been hurt himself. He knew it wasn't just the fault of Loren's husband. Loren had lied to him from the start, but Joe believed if Adrian had kept out of things then it would have turned out differently somehow.

Eventually Loren appeared online, only it wasn't her. Joe knew straight away it was Adrian using Loren's sign on. He asked Adrian what Loren's nickname was for him. Adrian said there was no nickname. In fact she had always called him a bastard wanker. Not the best nickname in the world but she had always meant it in good humour.

Joe told Adrian to cut the bull and get Loren to talk to him. Adrian wanted his chat account back. Joe simply logged off saying he would give it back once things between him and Loren were finally sorted.

The next day Joe wasn't surprised when Loren phoned him screaming like a banshee. He had expected nothing more than Adrian to go running to his wife.

He was distraught. Joe had no idea what to do. The woman had put him through so much over the last nine months. He had put his life on hold for the woman with her constant promises that things would eventually work out. How many times had she told him that when she was single they would be able to go out as a normal couple, that she would take him out and be the one to buy him dinner. He had put up with so much. He just couldn't get her out of his head. She had done this too many times before. It would have been okay he kept telling himself if she had just ended their relationship, as odd as it was, just the once, but no she always had to come back to him sooner or later. In the past he would calm down after a week or two and get on with his life, doing his best to enjoy his time with Reece despite Loren always being on his mind and the tears flowing freely when he was on his own. This time he couldn't sit back and do nothing as he had in the past. He went online to order flowers from an online florist. He had spoken to her husband, Adrian, who had no problem so it would seem with Joe sending his wife flowers. Adrian had Donna now so he didn't seem to care much about his wife and her bit on the side. That's all Joe had ever been after all; a married woman's fancy piece. He hated it but knew it was true even as he sat there credit card details in hand to order the bouquet of flowers. He didn't just stop at flowers though. Knowing how much the woman he loved liked flowers he ordered her a bottle of Champagne to go with it. Then when that got no response he ordered her more flowers and wrote her short love letters. He wanted nothing more than for all the silly games to end. Loren always came back. He was just tired of the constant waiting around for weeks. It had gotten worse over the last few months particularly since Adrian had found someone else to give his attention to other than his wife.

Still Joe had a bitter taste in his mouth when it came to Loren's husband. On that crazy night when she had taken the knife out to him over the stupid argument over the phone leading to them both spending a night in the cell, Adrian had sent Joe that rather childish message on chat smart telling him he had emotional problems and that things would never work out between them. The guy was obviously still jealous of whatever was between them, no matter how much he had insisted since that he wasn't. Sure he had Donna who he went to see in Sheffield at every opportunity he got but he still cared for, maybe even loved his wife. Joe knew this was only natural; after all they had spent most of their lives together so how could he not care for the woman? That much time together was something Joe could never fight. There would always be something between the two people that had caused him so much pain over what was fast approaching a year.

Loren did eventually call him. She thanked him for the flowers and the drink. She insisted it was over and that she wanted to be with nobody, which Joe found hard to believe as a few nights before the stabbing on her birthday she had indeed gone dancing with a man she had known online for what was apparently two years called Rueben. While after all the arguments had died down Joe no longer knew what to believe. All he knew for sure was that try as he might despite the assault then the stabbing, and finding out about other men no matter how innocent they may have been he still loved Loren. He felt trapped in a hell he had perhaps created himself. He should never have dated a married woman. He tried to convince her not to do what she always did which was to push him away. They eventually laughed about everything. He even spoke to Adrian who knew full well what Loren was like and that she always came back to Joe in the end. It didn't change anything. Loren was as stubborn then as she always had been the times before. Joe had heard every word that came out her mouth before. The requests for space she repeatedly told him, the lie that she didn't want or love him and that she just wanted a quiet life, to be on her own. Loren had no idea what love was. She couldn't explain her feelings for Joe. All he knew is that once upon a time as all fairy tales go she had told him she loved him on more than one occasion. Joe clung to that thought, those memories, with grim determination. She told him over and over again how she wanted nothing more than to sort her life out. Joe didn't believe a word of it. Loren would never get anything sorted. How many times had she done this to him before, nine, ten, he had lost count of the amount of times he had heard her say the exact same things only to call him after one too many glasses of wine telling him how sorry she was or that she missed him. After over an hour on the phone she hung up on Joe telling him that despite the fact she still cared for him and would miss him, and knew full well if they went out again they would enjoy each other's company as they were very much alike, it wasn't what she wanted. You don't know what you want Joe felt like telling her but bit his tongue, instead all he did was insist he wouldn't give up this time.

He didn't give up. It was inevitable that Loren would eventually come back.

Over the next few weeks Joe kept himself occupied with selling everything he had online. He continued to send Loren gifts despite her telling him not to. He sent several cases of white wine. He knew how much she loved her drink. The flowers went every other day not to mention more love letters in between. He bought her jewellery from gold earrings to necklaces all the while his heart aching with a loneliness he couldn't shake. After everything she had put him through he wished for nothing more than to be able to turn his back on her. He wished he had the strength to listen to his father when he had told him to keep away. It was like that time before Christmas when his father had told him never to give any woman one hundred percent until you could be sure they would return that same level of commitment. If she cared about you she would be here now, Joe remembered his father saying. His father had been right, but that didn't change anything. Joe had never felt a love so strong as the love he held in his heart for Loren. He thought it would be better if he hated her but knew he could not. She had continually lied to him. She had assaulted him and stabbed him, and yet through all that he just shrugged it off, letting his feelings carry him forward on a wave of persistence. He simply refused to give up.

Still there wasn't much else he could do. His actions were bordering on almost psychotic. He had no way of stopping himself from doing what he was doing and the money he was supposed to be using to save for a place for himself to rent was being dwindled away on gifts for Loren.

A week or two later Loren called him. She wanted to see him one last time to talk things through. They agreed to meet in Sutton Coldfield in the daytime so that they could sort things out. Joe thought that it was something they should have done a long time ago. Loren always seemed to call Joe when she needed him, usually after drinking too much wine, having argued with Adrian. He hoped this time they would resolve things one way or another.

They were supposed to meet in Sutton Coldfield town centre at nine thirty. Joe had no idea if Loren would actually show up his time. All she had said to him was that she had never let him down yet. In one way that was certainly true, she always turned up when and where she said she would. As far as letting him down went she seemed to have a habit of doing that. He had no way of contacting her as she had changed her mobile number yet again. He got to Sutton Coldfield early, very early at eight o'clock. He spent his time wandering around the place making his way to Hope Springs from the town centre then heading back again. It killed most of the time he had to spare. He popped into the local Argos store only to walk out again as he tripped over the mat in the door. He made a quick exit as the early morning shoppers simply gawped at him. He checked the time on his phone. It was ten past nine. He felt like he would be standing there until ten or eleven o'clock. If Loren didn't show he would go around the house. He was tired of the games she played with his mind. Luckily for Joe there was no need for him to go anywhere near the house as Loren called from a payphone ten minutes later.

"I'm in Sutton town centre. Where are you?" she asked him.

"I'm waiting outside the local Woolworths like you asked me to" he replied.

Loren had told him that there was a small café in the Woolworths store in Sutton Coldfield. There they would be able to have a cup of tea and a serious talk about the state of their relationship if there still was one. Joe had to concede that he didn't actually want to continue seeing her the way things were. He still loved her, but couldn't carry on unless Loren actually sorted her life out. He had heard her say the same old lines over again so many times he no longer believed her words. Joe hoped that in time she would prove him wrong. It just felt to Joe that as she had been married to Adrian for so many years the man had some kind of spell over her that she would never be able to break free of. Then there was the undeniable fact that Loren always admitted to. She never got around to doing anything. Joe doubted things could ever change.

Five minutes later she joined him outside Woolworths wearing bright orange baggy trousers, and an all too familiar brown top. He had taken the top off more times than he cared to remember at that point. It brought back memories of happy times they had spent together that he just couldn't think of in the same way anymore. The past had been tainted by so much bad feeling, so many lies. Joe wished then that he could just turn around to her tell her he hated her, walk away never looking back. He didn't have the courage of his thoughts. She offered him a cigarette smiling as they both lit up.

"I can't stop too long," she told him. "Adrian isn't very well, and I have to get back for the kids."

"Okay so we will smoke these and then go and have a talk inside," Joe replied as he smoked the cigarette she had offered him. They were Royals. Joe smoked them now too only because they reminded him of Loren. There was so much in his life that brought her to his mind he knew that he would never be able to shut her out. Giving up wasn't an option, but if things went well perhaps he could give her time. "I want us to have a proper talk," Joe insisted. "I know that you have feelings for me. I know a lot of bad things have happened. We have both said and done things we shouldn't have. But I have heard you say so much repeatedly. I don't want that today I want us to sort things out."

"Me too," said Loren

So they went inside going upstairs using the escalators to the small café. Loren ordered them both a cup of tea as Joe found them a table to sit at.

"So are we going to talk nicely?" Joe asked Loren as he poured the tea. They had been given two little metal tea pots full of tea together two teacups with saucers. Joe had fetched them some mini milk cartons as well as sugar.

"I'm not here to argue. This is about me and you. I don't want you messaging Adrian or that silly cow again."

"See you don't even care about Donna. This has never been about them it's about us. You tell me not to involve other people but that night you pulled the knife on me you involved my parents, not to mention my neighbours. They were all innocent people so let's not start placing blame."

Loren just looked at him as she slowly sipped her tea. She looked to Joe as good as she ever did if a little tired.

"I know you have feelings for me, and they aren't weak feelings," he told her. More than anything he felt frustration. He wondered if he could go back in time would he have done things differently. It was probably a question many people asked themselves when they reached a turning point in their lives when things were at their worst.

"I know I do. I never said they were weak either, but I don't love you." Loren replied seeming to be more focused on the hot drink in front of her than meeting Joe's eyes.

"You don't know what love is. You told me that yourself. You know what I think, I think you do love me but you can't understand it. That's why you always come back. You try to blame your drinking, but the booze isn't your problem. It's the stress. You used to stick to one bottle of wine a week." Joe reached over the table taking her hand in his.

"I know. It was leading to not one bottle though Joe but another and another. And I admit when I have a drink I go psycho that's why I need to sort myself out." Loren conceded. She couldn't look him in the eye as she admitted the truth to him.

"I know you do, but it's the same old story you never do. You have to do it or your life will never change."

"Things aren't great for me you know Joe. Adrian isn't well. He was supposed to go up to visit Donna in Sheffield this weekend. If he doesn't go I will have my back up. It may be the last time he sees her after all the trouble you caused. If he doesn't go I won't get any time to myself."

"We need to agree on something here. We can't keep going around in circles. I agree we shouldn't see each other, but you have your phone at work I think we should keep in touch that way."

"Sure I can do that, but no asking me in two or three weeks' time what I have done to sort things out. You need to concentrate on your own life. I can't call you all the time."

"I wouldn't want you to but when you're on a late shift you can call me. I wouldn't want you calling me when you're on an early I used to spend an hour each morning trying to get through to you. I was always on tender hooks."

"Ok then. So we will keep in touch and both get sorted. Deal?" Loren smiled at that as though she had Joe just where she wanted him. He would never figure her out. "Look I have to get back. It's been great seeing you. Both of us sober too." At that she got up to walk away.

Joe blocked her path, kissing her on the lips. "We aren't over," he told her firmly.

"Well for now we are on hold," she replied before turning her back and walking away.

Joe didn't say anything. He didn't know what to think. He just sat back down and watched as she slowly disappeared down the escalator. He sat there for a good ten minutes not really thinking about anything. He just sat sipping his tea. Then getting up he left the café, lit up a cigarette and made his way to the bus stop back home. He may never see Loren again. Still it was good to finally talk to the woman without a drink in her hand. Joe's life had been going in circles for ten months since he had met Loren it was time he made his own path walking a straight line for as long as he could manage.

EPILOGUE

Loren never called. Joe wasn't surprised at that. He had never really expected her to do as they had agreed that day. She was a free spirit who listened to no one and yet seemed to be influenced by everyone around her. The circle had been broken. Months passed with Joe having no choice but to walk the straight path he should have taken so long before. Getting involved with a married woman had been a mistake. Falling in love with one had been a disaster. In the movies things would work out just fine. Joe didn't have the luxury of celluloid all he had were the decisions he made. The consequences of his own actions had brought him to a point in his life where he had experience so much in a very short space of time. He was a changed man. More paranoid, more wary perhaps, but even so his life had been enriched by his heart's entanglement with Loren Green. He didn't look back on it as something bad. As the months continued to pass he made a success of himself with all the selling he had been doing online. He had learnt from his online trading experiences to a point where he could earn enough to quit his day job. He joined a gym once more taking it for what it was, a place to unwind and relieve the tension not a place to find new friends. He no longer chatted online. His time on the PC was purely for business. Whenever he did think of Loren though eventually in time that became less and less, he tried to remember all the good times they had shared, the wild nights of passion and the crazy online chats about everything under the sun. He no longer held out any hope that she would come back to him nor did it ever cross his mind that he would take her back. It had all been one big life experience. He never denied his feelings for her knowing that to fight his love would only cause him more pain. Instead he told himself mentally that it wasn't meant to be. If they had been soul mates thing would have worked out. The violent end made it clear to Joe, though it hadn't been so at the time, that there never could have been anything between them no matter how much he loved the woman. Sometimes hearts break. Eventually all hearts are mended no matter how battle broken. Life is full of surprises. For Joe Hughes, Loren Green had been the biggest surprise of his life. Who said all surprises had to be good?

THE END

ALSO BY Michael D McAuley

Sexy Soldier, Tasty Teacher Book 1 in the Naughty Knightley Series

The Feisty Fireman Tames the Teacher Book 2 in the Naughty Knightley Series

The Doctor's Lesson in Lust Book 3 in the Naughty Knightley Series

Made in the USA
Charleston, SC
05 September 2015